The Class

President's

Son

Written by:

Michael 'Petey' Powell

The Class President's Son

Copyright © 2013 by Bravin Publishing
Graphic design by 3906 Design, LLC
Photographs by T. Williams Photography
Edits by Whit Publishing Subsidiary of God's Gift, LLC
whitpublishing@gmail.com

ISBN: 978-0-9845018-9-2
Library of Congress Control Number: 2013930731

Bravin Publishing
PO Box 340317 Rochdale Village, New York 11434
www.bravinpublishing.com

Printed in the United States of America

DEDICATION

I dedicate this book to seven very special people...
My grandmother Mrs. Alma Powell.
My four wonderful children Maisha, Mia, Malik, Majid.
My beautiful mom, Melinda.
And my Dad, 'Big Mike'.

Thanks Grandma Alma for always believing in me and always knowing that I could be a legit business man. I will love you always. Rest in peace.

ACKNOWLEDGEMENTS

I want to thank my mom for being my rock, riding with me on my bid, and listening to me all those times over the phone. You're the world's number one mom. From the bottom of my heart, thank you. Pop, 'Big Mike', for remaining true to who you are; the realest man I know. Twenty years plus life, and you've kept your head and chin up. Salaam Pop's.

Uncle Lee, 'Big Dog', my partner in crime as the feds say (LMAO). I'm waiting on you to touch down Unc'. Coupes and suits await you. To Uncle Ty, out here with me; you taught me a lot Unc'. Things have changed out here but we made it. Love you Unc'.

Last, but certainly not least, Majid, Malik, Maisha, and Mia. Y'all are the reason I live and breathe. It's a blessing and a pleasure being your father. Stay smart.

Contents

INTRODUCTION

A few years ago in a little rural-'country' town in North Carolina, that till this day, less than two-thousand people live in, a few men in my family made millions on Red Bug Road. It's one of those towns that people really don't pay attention to. It sits right off Highway 74 East headed towards the coast. It's about forty miles from the Port City, a little over forty miles from I-95. Out of all the places I could have been raised, fate decided that Hallsboro was perfect for me. That's where I took my first steps, where the most memorable moments in my life happened, where I made my first million dollars and where I almost stopped believing in happily-ever-after...

I am Michael Powell; former federal inmate 55168066. This is my story. Most of the people that know me call me 'Petey'.

CHAPTER 1 – HUMBLE BEGINNINGS

I was only fifteen at the time, but I know I was looking at over half a million dollars spread out all over my pop's spacious bedroom. We tried as hard as we could, but me and my cousin Rooster were only able to count about ninety thousand dollars before we just gave up on the idea of counting it all...and there were still stacks of hundred dollar bills on my dad's California king-sized bed, on the bathroom counter, in his closet, all over the hardwood floor and everywhere else a rubber band-wrapped stack of money could fit.

At the time, Rooster and I were the same age. He'll end up signing a pro baseball contract, get shot in his leg and go to the feds (federal penitentiary) before the end of this story. As for my dad and the rest of us, you'll understand why sometimes I wish this was fiction.

At that particular time, that was the most money we'd ever seen. Between fantasizing about what I would do with it if it were mine, trying my best to slow down my heart rate so I wouldn't have an anxiety attack and blocking Rooster's grating voice out of my head because he was counting out loud; I could barely make it through a stack without having to recount it. All I could hear was Rooster counting to ten over and over, my father giggling at us and yelling at people down the hallway every few seconds, and Cameo, *'Just Like Candy'*, turned wide open down the hall.

There was candy everywhere. There was *'eye candy'* and a whole lot of *'nose candy'* at Pop's that day. His house was where everyone would hang out in Hallsboro. The 'dope boys', fine women, fiends, family, friends...pretty much everybody. If you ever heard about one of Big Mike's parties, you could bet that the most beautiful women you'd ever seen in your life were going to be there. There was free food, beer, liquor, reefer, coke; a smorgasbord of whatever you wanted. The only reason we even stopped by that night is he was having one of his parties. I was trying to catch him in a good mood, get a few dollars from him and leave. Dre was with me and Rooster that night – (God bless the dead). Dre ended up getting killed in a car accident in Bolton around '03. Bout this time he was a senior in high school and the only one of us with a license...I want to say that was '89.

When we pulled up to the house that night, there were cars parked on both sides of Red Bug and packed in my father's driveway. The smell of weed filled the air. It seemed like hundreds of people were spread all over the yard. Most of them were drinking and using. Some of them didn't even attempt to hide the fact that they were snorting cocaine. The house was a decent size with three bedrooms. At that time, it was one of the nicer homes in the neighborhood.

Rooster, Dre' and I could see folks partying their asses off as we got out of the car and walked towards the house. The loud music and the sound of people having a good time could be heard throughout the neighborhood, but that was normal. We already knew the house was packed with people, wall-to-wall, but there were a few of them in 'The Barn'. The Barn was a big three story building twenty yards behind the house. Pop always made everybody use the rear entrance of our home. Most people know my dad as 'Big Mike'.

In the end, the Feds gave my father a life sentence plus twenty years. You would think they found butt naked girls with masks and goggles on in 'The Barn' bagging up hundreds of kilos of coke right? That wasn't the case at all...

Fact #1: When the Feds charge you with a crime, they're going to accuse you of a whole lot more than you actually did-ALWAYS.

When you walked in the front door of 'The Barn' there was an office right under the stairs off to the right. It was only big enough for two or three people to fit in there and move around a little bit. There was a table in there and small digital scale hidden away in a teeny space right above the door. If you wanted work (drugs), that's where you got served.

There were two weight sets in the open-spaced first floor. On one side there was just a bench and a few dumbbells. Right across the room from that was the big universal weight set. There was also a television, radio, and a few chairs in there. The plywood walls were covered in black paint. In the beginning, bare plywood was all that was in there. My dad and my uncle just painted over them. Folks always came to work out, but there was a lot more weight getting pumped in the office than on the weight sets.

If you were able to go up to the second floor, you were privileged; just anyone couldn't go up there. There was a kitchen, a nice bar you could chit-chat at while you watched whatever was on the big screen, and a huge couch that sat right in the middle of the room. There was also a bedroom on that floor. It wasn't fancy at all, but it served its purpose. I can't begin to imagine how many women we took in and out of there.

The third floor was pretty much off limits. A few of us could go up there but everyone else just knew not to even look that way. It was an open space with a twin-sized bed centered against the far wall. At one point there were a lot of guns up there, over two hundred to be exact. My cousin and I had an arsenal of handguns, AR-15's, shotguns and just about every other kind of gun you can think of.

In every small town there's always going to be a lot of guns getting pawned in *'The Trap'* (dope spot) - people do a lot of hunting here in the south. Back then, most people who had pickup trucks had a shotgun or rifle sitting in the back window. You can't do that kind of thing in larger cities. There're more households with guns than households without 'em here. The census doesn't keep up with that kind of info. There was rarely a day that went by that different people weren't trying to trade us guns for coke when we were all hustling.

The feds claim *'The Barn'* was sort of like our headquarters, but really it was a spot my dad had behind his place that everybody just chilled at. Just-so-happened there was hustlers there most of the time, so we did what hustlers do.

On the night we tried counting all that money, Big Mike was being **BIG MIKE**. No matter where he was, my dad was always the life of the party. Till this day he's the most charismatic man I've ever encountered in my life, and the women loved it. When me, Rooster and Dre' walked into the house, Ms. Kathy was the first person we saw. She was one of my dad's friends who lived with him from time to time.

When my parents would separate, my mom would get an apartment in Whiteville, the next biggest town west of Hallsboro. Pop would let Ms. Kathy stay until my mother decided to come back home. Kathy was actually from the beach. He just kept her around for company, but I'd be lying if I said she wasn't fine.   Brown skinned, curvy, petite, with a flat stomach and short hair; kind of like Halle Berry's signature short hairdo. She warranted the attention of every eye within range. I never cared to get too involved with my dad's personal affairs, so I can't say that he was screwing her. To be honest, I really don't know.

She was high out of her mind that night; eyes blood shot red, but she still looked good as always. That 80's music my dad had playing through this expensive entertainment system he had was turned all the way up and she was walking around dancing with two wine glasses in her hands. She was playing the good hostess for the night. I remember nudging Rooster and getting him to look at that Kim Kardashian' when she was facing away from us. She had on a little black dress showing those almost perfect legs she had, the kind that doesn't really need stockings. I would always catch her early mornings working out in 'The Barn'. It was impossible to not stop and stare for a few seconds every time I saw her.

I didn't really like her, but my eyes did. I just didn't like the fact that she would always stay with my dad when he and my mom would split. I was pissed about that for years. It didn't really matter how many times I watched the Cosby show, I knew my family would never be like that.

Anyway, the party was jumping so the first thing we did was sneak a few beers out. It wasn't hard. All I did was grab a few out the cooler and give them to Dre so he could take them outside to the car and wait on us. People probably thought he was taking them to one of the older dudes outside. On top of that, I was Big Mike's son. No one had the balls to say anything to me any way. My Pop didn't play games, especially when it came to his money and his kids. As Rooster and I made our way through the house looking for my pop through all those people, I heard him calling us. ***"Petey, you and Rooster come back here."*** It seemed like he was in a good mood because his tone wasn't as forceful as it was when he usually called. He was standing at the end of the hallway by his room. Ms. Kathy was standing close to him trying to talk to him, but he wasn't really paying her any attention. He was focused on me and Rooster coming towards him. He had this serious look on his face. Big Mike was a shoot-it-straight dude, no chaser. I knew I wasn't in trouble, but that look meant hurry up.

As we got closer, he walked into the room and left Ms. Kathy standing there at the door. Her eyes just rolled up in her head in disgust. She quickly walked back towards the living room as me and Rooster followed behind my father into his room. My eyes got big as fifty-cent pieces, and before I could react to what I saw, it came flying out of Rooster's mouth...*"Oh S*#$@"!!!* Money was everywhere.

Big Mike closed the door behind us as soon as we walked and said *"If y'all can count it all out, you can have it. I know exactly how much it is, get to counting."*

Rooster jumped right on it- No plan of how we were going to count it all or nothing. My father always meant what he said, so Rooster knew he wasn't playing about knowing exactly what was in there. He also knew that if we counted all that paper, my father might have actually given it to us. That's the kind of man he was, one who kept his word. The look on my dad's face went from being somewhat serious, to one of those sneers that said, 'Its-going-to-be-funny-as-hell-wathching-these-boys-try-to-count-this-money' looks. He opened the door and stood in the doorway looking down the hall. He would look at us for a little while, then glance down the hall into the living room and yell something to one of the people partying. Only a few people could come down the hallway, my uncles, cousins, you know...people who were real close to him.

I'm not going to sit here and make you think there was five hundred thousand on the line for us; I was just there to get a few dollars. Rooster on the other hand, thought we actually had a chance of getting all that money. I ended up getting about three hundred dollars from Big Mike that night. He gave Rooster and Dre' about twenty-five a piece. I can smile about it now but really, thinking back, I don't have a clue about the reason he had all that money in his room that night. Me and the boys went out, but when I got home that next morning, 'Big Mike' was sleeping like a baby in that room. There wasn't a sign the money had ever been there. Ms. Kathy was sleep on the recliner in the living room. The house was a mess, but by the time I woke up later that day, it was like none of those people ever came. Ms. Kathy would always wake up early and clean up after those parties. After she finished, she would go straight to the barn and work out a little. She never missed a workout, no matter how screw-faced she got the night before.

Big Mike had great relationships with everybody; a real people person, but I've never been fishing with him. That's one of those things that most fathers in the south do with their kids. I've been a phenomenal athlete since little league, and I can't really remember him coming to too many of my games. He was there, provided more than enough, and I know he loved me; I guess that's really the only thing that matters at the end of the day. 72% of black kids are raised by a single parent. Guess you could say I was one of the lucky ones. My father was constantly busy and always on the move. There was even one year that I only saw him twice; but he was around-he was there.

My grandmother, Alma, and grandfather, Emory, a man of few words that ran his ship with an iron fist, were hard workers and raised 4 boys on Red Bug Rd. My grandfather worked hard all of his life and was able to provide a descent lifestyle for his family. To be totally honest, my grandparents were on the lower side of middle-class.

The oldest was my uncle Melvin, now, he's Dr. Melvin Powell. Unc got into the school system after he graduated from college and went on to become a school principal. He was actually my principal at Hallsboro Elementary School, right up the street from my grand-parent's home. I hated every second of it. Uncle Melvin was cool and did a great job as the principal, but I always felt like he was way too hard on me. All the teachers knew he was my uncle, and if they had any problems out of me, they would take me straight to his office. I didn't get the special treatment you'd think I would. Whatever the harshest punishment was for whatever I did was exactly what I got.

Then there was Uncle Charles. Everybody has always called him 'Darby' for as long as I remember. He turned out real good. He and his wife have a nice-sized church in Whiteville now. Everyone in the county adores them. Who wouldn't love a husband and wife that preach together?

I love all my uncles, but the closest to my heart is Uncle Ty. I've met a lot of people in my 38 years, but Tyrone Powell is without a doubt the realest dude I've ever encountered; other than my father. He started hustling early on in his life. See there were a lot of boot-leggers in Hallsboro when my uncles and pops were growing up. Rural North Carolina was known for its liquor houses in those days. There were multiple liquor houses in every small town that were bringing in a few dollars. We had about 5 or 6 in Hallsboro then, but Bubba Shaw's was the hot spot. You could go over there and have a drink, gamble, listen to old school music, get a little weed or whatever-that's where a lot of folks spent their evenings. That's where Ty perfected his craft; hustling.

Uncle Ty started making money when he was about 13 or 14-years-old. His first hustle was liquor. He would get someone to go into town and buy him a few pints, and then he would give them to the older guys on credit until they got paid. He charged them dou-ble-whatever he paid per pint. Most of them did farming work or other odd jobs that didn't pay too well. Poverty was everywhere you looked.

Around 15, Ty started hustling weed. He still would help my granddad and people around Hallsboro crop tobacco and farm, but liquor and weed kept a little money in his pocket. Unc was making money way before the crack era started. Once he started, he never stopped, and the thought of slowing down never crossed his mind.

Then there was 'Big Mike', my dad. Pops was pretty much the all-around guy. He was the most charismatic of all the boys, one of the best athletes Hallsboro had ever seen, and was undoubtedly one of the smartest of my grandparent's kids. He'd been a ladies man since a little boy, and his school grades were way above average. Big Mike was the class president of his graduating class. A lot of people tell me he made straight A's throughout most of his schooling. With the charm he had, the grades, and the fact that he was an all-star athlete, you would have thought he would have went off to college at one of the more prestigious universities when he graduated. That's the thing about life, everybody knows things don't always go the way everybody thinks they should.

My father met one of the most beautiful women I've seen in my life right before he graduated. This gorgeous young lady, Melinda Wilson from Whiteville, had a newborn baby girl named Tracy. She simply blew his mind. Out of all the women he dealt with when he was in high school, she was the only one who had his heart, and he gave her all of it. Everyone in my family says they were inseparable. A little over a year after they met and fell in love, she became pregnant-with me. I was born in '74.

My granddad raised his boys to be real men and to take care of their responsibilities, so when my mom got pregnant; my dad got a full time job at a local plant named National Spinning. He worked his ass off and stayed there for a little while, but back then all the

men in the area were trying to get on at DuPont. DuPont was everybody's dream job. They had great pay, benefits, and it wasn't too
far from home. Coming from a small little town like Hallsboro, getting on at DuPont was like hitting the lottery. When he got on there,
he was able to get a home right beside my grandparents on Red bug.
When I say right beside my grandparent's...if me and my sister were
running through the hallway of our house playing too loud, my
grandmother would call and tell my mother to make us quiet down
a little bit. DuPont is where my dad's life took a turn for the worst
to be honest with you.

Here's how it was told to me...

See, my dad was a real personable character. People were
drawn to him everywhere he went. Didn't matter if we were at a
cookout or the grocery store, people would always find a reason to
start a conversation with him. I'm justified in saying he mastered
the art of conversation.   He knew a little bit about everything.
There wasn't a topic you could engage him with that he didn't know
anything about, at least I've never seen it happen. Didn't take long
for 'Big Mike' to get popular at DuPont. I remember him always
telling my mom and Uncle Ty about all these different people at
work. When we went to the mall or other places in Wilmington, we
would always run into someone from his job. Each person we saw
would almost always come and have a conversation with my dad.

Everyone, especially my grandma, always said that Bike Mike was a star everywhere he went.

Living beside my grandparents helped out a lot. My father worked a swing shift, mostly nights, and my mom would always manage to maintain nursing and factory jobs. Me and my sister Tracy would go between babysitters and my grandparent's. In the early years my mom was able to spend a lot of time with us but as we got older she worked a lot more.

Big Mike drank and smoked a little weed, but it was more of a recreational thing for him. A few times out of the week, him and a few guys from the neighborhood would get together, have a few drinks and smoke a little. Uncle Ty would be around him every now and then, but most of the time Unc was somewhere hustling weed or anything else he could get his hands on. After a few months at

DuPont, Pop got real acquainted with how things worked. He knew which managers were cool, which ones where dick heads, who was sleeping with who; he was pretty much hip to everything that was going on. That's how he was.

When he got paid, he would always buy weed to smoke. Not much, maybe a half ounce or ounce. He would smoke a little and sell a little. A few guys around the neighborhood would buy a couple joints or a couple small bags from him, and a few people from his job would cop from him too.

The guy he was getting it from actually worked with him. Him and Big Mike started working at DuPont around the same time, and got cool. He and my dad would smoke joints on their breaks. When he told my dad that he had it (weed), Pop just dealt with him from that point. He would always look out for my dad. No one could touch his prices with a ten foot pole. Not too many people at the job knew that the dude was hustling. He was real private, but he and my dad were just cool. He was selling out of his house in Leland, but no one at work would have ever guessed. You never know what people do behind closed doors.

Uncle Ty was still in high school then selling weed, liquor, and cigarettes. When he found out Big Mike was getting good weed for cheap, he wanted some. At first, my dad would give him a little to sell. At the same time, Pop was selling a little at home and a little at work. Before long, they would put their money together to get big-ger quantities. When the word started getting around that they had the good weed, people began hunting them down to get it.

Pop worked the night shift and sold a few bags on his breaks. When his shift was over he would serve out of his car in the parking lot. Uncle Ty was getting his off in school and around the neigh-borhood. People knew my father would usually sleep during the day, but they didn't care. All day, different people would stop by to get weed from him; mostly people from work. He was hardly getting any sleep, but he never complained about them coming all throughout the day.

This white guy, Aaron B., stopped by from time-to-time. Aaron was a little younger than my dad, but they were pretty cool. His father, Ellis B., sold weed too. When Big Mike's connect at work wouldn't have anything, Ellis would always have what Big Mike needed. And when Ellis would run out, Big Mike was always able to serve him. Between my dad, Uncle Ty, and Ellis...I don't think there was ever a drought (shortage of weed) from Hallsboro to Wilmington.

That went on for a few years and then Bernard showed up. He was from Hallsboro, but was living in Rocky Mount at the time. He would stop by every now and then when he was in town to shoot the breeze with Uncle Ty and my dad. Bernard had made a name for himself selling weed in the Rocky Mount-Roanoke Rapids area, but he was blown away by how much money Ty and my dad were making right there in Hallsboro. Pop didn't want to deal with him because he thought Bernard was a little too flashy and talkative. Big Mike didn't really care about people knowing he was hustling, but he didn't want anybody knowing where he was getting it from. I'm not too sure what happened, maybe my dad's connect and Ellis didn't have anything at that particular time, but one day Ty and Big Mike hit the highway headed to Rocky Mount...

CHAPTER 2 – THE ALLURE

There's not a whole lot of intellect involved in selling drugs. Regardless of how intelligent the biggest drug dealers on the planet seem, there's a very simple principle to taking over the market in any particular area.

Sell the best quality and quantity for the cheapest price

When Big Mike and Uncle Ty came back from Rocky Mount, they were able to do just that. Bernard wasn't lying when he told my dad and Uncle Ty that he had it. At the price they were able to purchase marijuana for from Bernard, they were able to increase their market share. They sold more for less and gave their customers just a little bit more than the competition gave. On top of that, they were nice guys; people persons. It didn't take long for the news to travel that they had the best weed around and had the biggest bags. They made that trip to Rocky Mount a few times a week, and more and more customers came. Soon after, my dad and Uncle Ty started supplying Ellis B. and my dad's connect at work. Their business kept getting bigger and bigger.

After a few years, Bernard introduced them to a guy named Donald Ray in Rocky Mount. From what I've heard, Donald Ray was a multi-millionaire way back in the late seventies. He had small legal businesses, but he was a king in the weed game. Donald Ray was one of the biggest weed suppliers from South Carolina to Richmond, V.A. He took a liking to my dad and Uncle Ty, and that's when business really started booming.

Meanwhile at home, things weren't so good. My mom hated all the traffic that was coming to the house, and everything else that had anything to do with my dad hustling.

My father sold weed to some of the most prominent business owners and community figures around. The good thing about his relationships with them was the fact that he could keep large quantities of weed at their establishments. Think about it...the police wouldn't dare raid a police officer's home or a school teacher's home back in those days. Big Mike would pay some of the most unsuspecting people to keep drugs on property. He was still working all night during the week and selling weed all day. What wife in her right mind wouldn't get tired of that?

Pop smoked weed and drank; Uncle Ty smoked weed and drank, but Pop started doing a little coke and turned into straight party animal. He and my mom would argue all the time about him staying out all night on the weekends. I can't begin to tell you how many times I would wake up on Saturday mornings to the tune of my mom fussing him out for coming home after the sun was up. She wasn't the least bit timid about going at it with him. As soon as he came in the front door from a night of partying, she was scream-ing. A lot of times, it would get so bad that my Grandmother would overhear them arguing and come over. It was really a blessing that my grandparents stayed so close. Regardless of how bad it got, when Grandma showed up she would calm both of them down pret-ty quickly. Grandma wouldn't ever say much, but when she walked in, both of them got as quiet as church mice. My sister and I would just stay in our rooms. I don't know what she was doing in hers, but I remember a whole lot of mornings I would just lay in my bed star-ing at the ceiling hoping they would just stop.

Big Mike and my mom loved each other dearly, but it's no se-cret that their marriage was plagued by separations. The first time my mom and dad separated was when I was in head start. Me, my mom, and Tracy ended up moving into an apartment in Whiteville. My parents made the decision to move me back to Hallsboro when I was in the first grade. I lived with my grandparents that year, and my parents ended up getting back together the following year. Me, my mom, my dad, and my sister were all together again as a family.

Fact: Children Don't Have a Say-so in what environment they're raised in

My dad was partying all over the place from Raleigh to Charlotte to Wilmington, but he really loved Atlantic Beach. My grandmother was from down there, so we had a lot of family there. Big
Mike loved to party at my cousin Ronell's spot down
there,'Cadillacs.' That's also what everybody called Ronell. 'Cadillac's' was a little after hours spot right on the ocean, and a whole lot
of people hung out there late nights. It didn't close till seven or
eight in the morning, and when Big Mike went down there-he usually was the last person to leave with Cadillac. Hanging out there
was real cool because my Pop knew most of the people in the area.
He'd been back and forth from the beach to Hallsboro all of his life.

My grandma always loved going down there to visit her sisters,
and would take all of her kids with her when she would go. It had
always been like a second home to my Dad and Uncle Ty, so of
course it was quite natural for them to hustle there. A lot of times
my cousin 'Manager' would hang out at Cadillac's with my dad.
They were tight since they were kids. Most times my father hung
out at the beach, he would stay with one of them down there and
not come home until late the next day. Every single time, my mom
would argue with him before he left, and go postal on him when he
came home. Even though the arguments were always intense, they
never lasted too long. All the bills at home were paid, both my parents drove nice cars, my sister and I were well taken care of, and my
father was making a lot of money. At any given time at that point,

my dad would have thirty to forty grand in cash stashed in the house. That kind of money makes it real tough for a woman to just walk away from.

Uncle Ty didn't care too much for a whole lot of partying. He would rather stay in Hallsboro and make money than go out and spend a bunch of cash he didn't have to. Since I can remember, he's always had a keen eye for money making opportunities and always took full advantage of those opportunities. Uncle Ty probably did a little cocaine, but he didn't make it a habit like my dad did. Ty saw cocaine as another opportunity to make money. There weren't a whole lot of people that did cocaine then because it was a little expensive, but the people who were able to buy it had a few dollars. In the late seventies-early eighties, coke was one of those drugs that represented status. Uncle Ty and my father were making around $5,000 a week with weed sales so selling cocaine was naturally the next step.

One of those nights that Big Mike was about to go out really sticks out like a sore thumb in my head. As usual, my mom's attitude got really salty when my dad started getting dressed. My sister and I were up watching TV in the living room. We both usually got a little quiet during these times because we knew the argument was coming. The reason this time sticks out is because while we were sitting there someone knocked on the door. I had to go get my mom to open it, because if we would have, my mother and father would have had our asses. Our parents never let us answer the door; that was the rule. If we knew it was our grandma or someone like that, it was cool, but we would get our behinds tore up if we ever answered that door for anybody else.

My mom didn't like the fact that someone was coming to the house that late and when she was on her way down the hallway to see who it was, I remember her saying, ***"Who the hell is that knocking on my damn door!!!"*** She said it loud enough for my dad and whoever was outside to hear. She wasn't in a good mood at all, and jerked the door open. To be honest I thought she was going to curse whoever it was out, but when she saw them she just calmed right on down and started laughing; it was Uncle Ty. ***"Ty you know you like to got it right?"*** She said it jokingly and walked back to her bedroom. I'm assuming she was going back to ask my dad a million questions about where him and Ty were going that night.

We all loved Uncle Ty, especially my sister and I. He always went out of his way to give us attention. We lit up like jack-o-lanterns every time we saw him and like always, he reached in his pocket and gave us some money. It was never much, maybe fifty cent or a dollar a piece. We were real young so it felt like a million. We thought Uncle Ty was filthy rich because he always had some-thing to give us; money, candy, a little toy or something he picked up from the store-always. My mom didn't really give my dad a hard time when he and Ty were headed out that night. Maybe it's because she didn't want to cut up in front of Uncle Ty, but whatever it was; she was a whole lot calmer.

Big Mike and Ty made their way to the beach that night. As usual, Big Mike ended up at 'Cadillac's'. Ty would hang out at the beach a lot too, but he spent most of his time there selling weed. He would hang out at 'Cadillac's' from time to time when he was down there, but it was mostly business.

I fell asleep on the couch that night watching TV, and was awaken by the sound of my Dad and Uncle Ty in the kitchen. I was half-asleep walking into the kitchen to see them. When I got to the kitchen door I saw small little plastic baggies all over one side of the table, and my dad was using a small measuring spoon to put cocaine in one of them. He didn't notice me standing there, but Unc did.

He said **"Petey go on in your room and go to sleep little man"**, as he got up from the chair and walked towards me. My dad couldn't get up fast because his hands were full, but he wasn't too happy that I had seen what they were doing. All I remember him saying was **"Petey, go get your butt in that bed!"** Uncle Ty picked me up and carried me to my room door. Knowing Uncle Ty, he probably promised me some candy or a toy or something to go ahead and get in the bed and go to sleep. At that age, maybe around 7 or 8, candy or a toy was all it took for me to be happy.

When they started selling cocaine, everything changed. My dad didn't stop working the night shift at DuPont, and he didn't slow down selling weed at all, but a whole lot of new faces started popping up-and a whole lot more money. Sleeping during the day was always hard for him because of the steady traffic coming to buy weed, but the cocaine traffic was way worse. Between my dad and Uncle Ty being up the street, Red Bug starting slowly looking like a constant parade. Some mornings when Big Mike would come home from work, he would just fall asleep in his car sitting in the driveway. A lot of times, my mom, me, or my sister would go outside and wake him up if he slept too long. He didn't do that all the time, but it happened every once in a while.

Uncle Ty on the other hand was constantly traveling back and forth from Hallsboro to the beach. He always had a room inside my grandmother's home, but he also would rent apartments at the beach and sometimes around Hallsboro. Both, my dad and Uncle Ty, hustled during the day, but while my dad was working at DuPont at nights, Ty was out in the street getting money nonstop.

In those days Tracy and I spent most of our time at my grandparent's house. After we grew out of the toddler stage my mom went back to work fulltime; all the time. My mother loved to work. She was far from lazy and regardless of how much money my dad was making, she always had her own.

With them the arguments became more frequent, mostly because my dad was always gone. During the week he worked at night, slept a little but hustled a lot more during the day. During the weekends he partied like a rock star. My mom tried the best she could to hold it together, my grandmother would even spend countless hours begging her to stay and work things out, but every now and then she just couldn't take it.

He was always busy. If he wasn't working, he was hustling. If he wasn't hustling, he was out partying. If he wasn't out partying, he was sleep. I spent a lot of those days at my grandmother's and wouldn't go home until nightfall. My cousin Ann would babysit me and Tracy during the day. She lived there with my grandparent's and would always get stuck babysitting us until my grandma got home in the evening. She was a teenager at the time. We would play all day, and I would always go out and play with the other kids in the neighborhood. Most times they would be playing on the church yard across the street from my grandmother's house. When my grandmother would get home from work, she would spoil the hell out of me. Throughout my entire life, until her dying day, my grandmother was my best friend. She would cook as soon as she got home, and I would be right up under her. Most times, she would cook two meals a day. She would cook the same exact thing every day for my grandfather; fish. That man ate fish every day for years and years. Don't ask me why, I have no idea, but that's exactly what he wanted. Then, she would cook a meal for everyone else. She smiled the entire time and never complained about it.

Uncle Ty was always in and out of the house, but he would always spend time with me. Ty always worked out and had a weight set around my grandparents, so I would lift weights with him when I was real young. I wasn't lifting anything heavy at all, but I was lifting. The neighborhood park was right up the street, so we would go up there often to play basketball. He taught me everything there was to know about the game, and didn't mind spending hours out there teaching me. While we were out there people would come up to buy weed or cocaine from him.

When he would go to the store or anywhere else, I was usually sitting right there in the passenger seat. Back in those days Uncle Ty loved to smoke weed, so it was normal for him to light up a joint as soon as he got in the car.

Pop just couldn't stay home on the weekends to save his life. It got to the point that my mom didn't even get upset anymore, but then he started taking trips. That man would be in New York one weekend, Washington, D.C the next weekend, Florida the next weekend; he would be all over the place. He would be visiting some of our family or some of his friends, but the real fact-of-the-matter is...he was meeting new cocaine connects everywhere he went.

Most times when he got back in town on Sunday evenings, Uncle Ty would come to the house as soon as he got there or my dad would meet him. None of those trips out of town were just to visit. It was all business. Big Mike was bringing back big cocaine.

The word on the street traveled fast. Everyone knew that my dad and Uncle Ty had some of the best coke around, and the traffic came. Some days Pop had to call into work because the traffic had grown to the point where it was literally impossible for him to sleep.

As for me, I was starting to fall in love with sports. Right after school I would run down to the park and play basketball until nightfall. I had the best coach in the neighborhood, Uncle Ty, so I was one of the best kids out there playing.

The first time I got the chance to play organized sports was around 8-years-old. It was a basketball league that they got together at Hallsboro High School. A white gentleman named Mike Mobley was my first coach. He may have been in his mid-30's around then. Mike was one of the best baseball players to ever come out of this area, drafted straight out of high school to play pro. After playing ball a number of years, fate moved him to Hallsboro to work with youth in sports in our little town. Our first encounter wasn't the nicest...

A bunch of us were running a game in the gym, and being that young, hardly any of them could actually dribble the ball, shoot, or nothing. I was a superstar because Uncle Ty had already schooled me to the game. In the middle of our game, Mike came up and started playing with the team that my little squad was playing against. I was advanced and my team was killing the other team, but this grown man decided to help them out and they started winning. Even then I was extremely competitive, so I was pissed off. I was trying to guard him, but I was yelling and screaming at him at the same time. *"Get yo' old self out the way!"*

I walked up on him mad and puffed up. I wasn't what you would call a good kid back then; my attitude was bad as hell, excuse my French, but that's what it was. I calmed down a little when I found out that he was the guy running the league, and one of the other coaches talked to me. The other coach was one of Uncle Ty's best friends, Mr. Robinson.

Mike was a great guy and saw a lot of potential in me. When the basketball league's season was over, he ended up coaching Dixie Youth Baseball. It was only right that I played on his team. He would always work with me after practice and when he gave me rides home, he really took the time to explain to me that sports could take me places. Pop rarely showed up to the games, but Uncle Ty was there most of the time. Coach Mobley ended up playing a huge role in my life.

When the crack era came, Big Mike and Uncle Ty were already making a killing; somewhere in the range of ten to fifteen grand a week from what I've been told. A few of my cousins at the beach were already getting to the money along the same time my dad and Uncle Ty were coming up. That beach traffic was insane compared to the traffic coming through Hallsboro. With all the tourists and people that frequented the beach from surrounding areas, they were damn-near millionaires before crack really flooded the south. Pop and Unc had an opportunity to see its money-making potential before they ever laid hands on it. They also had an opportunity to see how it was cooked, packaged, and sold. They became experts before they played the game...

CHAPTER 3 – THE CUBAN CONNECTION

Big Mike was always complaining about working at DuPont. It went from being a means of supporting his family to a 'front' to justify his income, especially when he reached the point that the money he was making in the street was a whole lot more than he was making at work. When he and Unc started turning cocaine into crack...well, you know how it went from there.

When they started selling crack, they had no idea what was about to happen. The crack customer was a different animal; it's addictive nature was something out of this world. People started stealing, pawning and prostituting. Crack had been around, but when they started selling it, that's the type of people that came around. Crack fiends were hanging out all day and all night around the neighborhood. They were walking up and down Red Bug, sitting around at the park, at the liquor houses. Sometimes when my mom would have me and my sister in the car coming home at night, we would usually pass by a whole bunch of fiends walking Red Bug. Most of the women walking were tricking (prostituting). Wasn't like they were trying to hide it, they were all out in the open hopping in and out of cars. A few break-ins happened around

Hallsboro, but never anywhere close to our side of Red Bug. More customers came, and they kept coming and coming back; all times of the day and night. Pop, Uncle Ty, and their crew were making money hand over fists.

There's a viscous rumor that's been going around for years about how the 'Powell Boys' started making big money. It's kinda funny to us; we've just never been that type of people. But rumor has it that my pop, Uncle Ty, and a few of their goons went down to Miami and robbed and killed the leader of a huge South American drug cartel. Sounds like the makings of a blockbuster film huh? That rumor is so far from the truth its crazy, but there was a Cuban...

We'll get to what really happened in a few paragraphs...

Big Mike got hurt playing basketball and had to have surgery on his knee in the early 80's. In those days, a lot of doctors weren't real savvy with cosmetics when it came to body parts like the knee, so he had this big scar that ran from the bottom of his thigh down to the top of his shin. My dad was in excruciating pain all the time. The meds would make him feel a little better, but cocaine numbed him out. Seems like the more pain he was in, the more coke he snorted. I guess it was a good thing for his customers, because he was always in search of the best product.

He complained about DuPont every single day after his surgery. By this time, Red Bug was on fire. Uncle Ty and my dad had non-stop traffic coming from all over. People were coming from Wilmington, Leland, the Beach, all over the county, you name it. They and a few of their guys were selling crack, coke, and weed all throughout Hallsboro-the park, all the liquor houses, a few houses in the community and at home. We didn't have a police department and you rarely ever saw a county sheriff ride through. Ty and my dad were slowly turning Red bug into the cocaine capital of southeastern North Carolina.

As for me when I was younger, I had other plans. Mike Mobley embedded the idea in my head that I could actually become a professional athlete, and that's what I truly believed I was going to do. Every chance I got I was playing basketball, baseball, or football with the kids in the neighborhood or in the organized leagues. I wasn't just taking up space on the bench; I was a stand out in every sport I played. On top of being good, I was the most popular kid on every team I played for because of my family. I was a little arrogant, but I backed it up with my performances every time I stepped on the court or on the field.There's some truth to the rumor that our big break came from Miami, but my dad never murdered any cartel kingpins. Big Mike, as always, went on one of his weekend rendezvous. I was around ten at the time, and vividly remember my dad being excited about going down to Miami. He talked about it for weeks before he left. I remember Uncle Ty joking about it with him leading up to the time he was about to leave. Ty was saying things like, ***"Mike, you ain't goin' down to no Miami. Miami Vice goin' be on you as soon as you get in the city limits."*** My dad always did what he said so Unc knew he was going but he joked with him anyway. See, my dad had this big idea that he could go down there and find a big coke connect. That's exactly what he did, went down there and somehow found 'Julio'; The Cuban.

Pop drove down there one weekend and hooked up with some dope boys (drug dealers) that one of his connects at the beach put him on. They met up, but at the time, they couldn't fill the whole order and the price they were trying to sell what they did have for was way too high. No real hustler likes to miss money, so they took Big Mike to meet up with this Cuban guy, Julio. Julio was a short and stocky Cuban man who honestly looked like a migrant worker. Mike thought Julio was just a front man for somebody because the guy didn't look like he had two nickels to his name, and drove an old beat up van to meet up with them. Julio couldn't speak good English, but the dope boys that carried Big Mike to meet him could understand him perfectly fine. He would speak a few words in broken English, and then he would slip up and say a few Spanish words. He used his hands a lot when he talked. Every time he had to speak English it was a struggle, but he had a lot of coke; and I do mean A LOT.

Before my dad left home to go down there, him and Unc put together about one hundred-fifty thousand dollars for Big Mike to buy coke with. When Julio told my dad that he was delivering kilos up to Virginia every few weeks, he knew it wasn't going to be a problem for him to stop by Hallsboro on his way.

Julio was selling kilos for eighteen-thousand, and that was cheaper than anybody my dad has ever dealt with was able to let a thousand grams (kilo) go for. Big Mike wanted five of them, but there was one problem. Julio had this thing about wanting to see where the people he dealt with lived before he sold them anything. There wasn't anything wrong with that. It was the easiest way to make sure he wasn't dealing with an undercover, but the thing was, he wanted Big Mike to give him half the money up front. He wanted the other half when he came with the coke. Mike wasn't trying to hear it at first, and that didn't seem to bother Julio at all. He was doing too much business to worry about one person only buying five kilos.

For as long as I can remember, my dad has always been a risk taker. The worst thing that could have happened was that he would have been out of a lot of cash if he would have given Julio the money and Julio didn't come through. Pop wasn't going to spend a whole bunch of time down in Miami and not come back without what he went down there for, so he gave Julio fifty-thousand dollars and came back home. He figured if he gave Julio five-thousand more than he asked for up front, Julio would see that he was serious about his business.

I remember the day he got home like it was yesterday. He got in a few hours before he had to go to work. Me and my sister were watching television in the living room when we heard his car pull up outside. I walked over to peep out the blinds to make sure it was him. I saw my Pop just sitting there in the car, but I also saw Uncle Ty and Spike walking down the driveway towards him. They walked over from my Grandmother's house. Spike and my dad have always been best friends, but they're actually first cousins. For as long as I can remember, Spike has been a straight comedian-always sarcastic; saying something funny as hell. He and my dad were the same age and both of them would have taken a bullet for each other. They worked with each other at DuPont, so sometimes they would carpool.

I cracked the front door about to walk out the house to speak to my father and I remember him telling me to stay inside. "I'll be in there in a second son." Big Mike was actually out there telling Uncle Ty and Spike about Julio and giving him the money. You would think that Uncle Ty would have gotten upset at the fact that Big Mike gave someone fifty-thousand without getting the coke from him right then, and actually believing that the guy would drive all the way up from Miami to North Carolina to deliver right? That wasn't the case at all. After my dad finished explaining, Uncle Ty gave him a blank stare for a few seconds and told him what he was thinking.

"So Bruh, you really feel good about this guy?" Ty asked, with a tilted head, squinted eyes and a puzzled look on his face. After Ty asked, Pop just shook his head and said yea. *"Well, the only thing we can do is wait and see if he come. Worse thing that can happen is we out of fifty grand. If the joker does show up, hey, we got a plug."* Ty said. Uncle Ty trusted my dad's judgment, always. Spike on the other hand, always gave my dad hell. Not in a bad way, he just always picked with him.

Spike sarcastically said *"Now Mike, next time you take yo' ass down to Miami, make sure I go with you so you won't do nothing stupid like that no more. That man probably half way to Cuba with that money smoking a big ole' joint by now."*

The only thing that had my dad and Uncle Ty scared was the fact that they didn't know when he was coming. They knew it was going to be in the next few days, but they didn't know exactly when. That night my dad and Spike went to work. Before he left for DuPont, he told us that he was expecting an important phone call.

He was adamant about us not tying up the phone line and real clear about clicking over if we were on the phone and there was a beep.

That next morning when he got home, the first thing he asked was whether or not someone called. We told him no but he asked again, ***"Yall ain't have the phone lines tied up did you? Yall sure that phone ain't ring?"*** You would have thought he was waiting on a call from the president.

Big Mike had Julio's number, but he didn't want to seem too anxious so he didn't call. It's not like he didn't want to, Uncle Ty just suggested it wouldn't be a good look. Unc has always demonstrated an incredible amount of patience. He and my dad are night and day when it comes to that; my dad didn't like waiting on nothing.

Big Mike was uptight that whole week. He didn't really talk to any of us, he kept peeping out the blinds every time he heard a car passing by or pulling in the driveway, he called into work a few times, he was rude to almost everybody who came to the house buying coke from him; he was a hot mess.

A few days went by, and then it happened. An old beat up van pulled into the driveway. My sister and I were on the way from my grandparent's house that evening. We knew a lot of the people that came to the house to buy from my father, but this van, we'd never seen it before. Right when we walked pass it in the driveway, Pop came outside and quickly walked towards it smiling from ear to ear. That was the first time I saw Julio.

Tracy and I went inside, but as soon as we made it into the house, we saw my mom inconspicuously standing by the living room window looking through the open blinds. *"Who's that your dad out there talking to?"* she asked softly while she peered through the blinds. We didn't know. Big Mike stood out there talking for a few minutes, that's when Julio and another guy stepped out of the van. The other guy was short and stocky as well, but he was a whole lot darker than Julio. That was Julio's brother, Paquito. Both of them resembled the migrant workers who did farm work in the area. The thing that always stuck out about Paquito for years to come is the fact that he spoke English well and carried a big gun on his waist-a big .357 magnum.

Paquito did most of the talking. He was pretty much Julio's translator. They stood out there talking to Big Mike for a while before they ended up pulling the van behind our house. My dad came inside and my mom started asking him a million questions. *"Who are those people? Why they pulled up behind the house like that? Mike what you got going on back there?"* My dad gave her one answer that summed up his response to everything she asked. *"Why you all in my damn business? You ain't got nothing to do with nothing going on out there."* He was walking to his room as fast as he could, so he really didn't care to speak to her at the time. Pops was going to his stash to get the other forty grand. Big Mike had a few stash spots around the house. It wasn't strange at all for us to be cleaning the house and find twenty or thirty grand under a dresser, in a closet, or wherever- it happened all the time. While Pop was going to his stash, Julio and Paquito were hard at work in our backyard taking the dashboard out of that raggedy van. That's where they always stashed the coke they came with.

When Big Mike gathered the money from his stash, he walked outside and told them to come into the backroom of the house when they finished. That room was on the back of the house, but it was sectioned off from the rest of the house. Mike would serve his customers through there, because it kept them from coming inside and away from us.

It took them forever to get that dashboard down. When they finished, they went inside and laid the five kilos in front of Big Mike on the table that sat in the middle of the room. Pop snorted some like he always did, and felt that freeze that everybody who snorts coke looks for. This time, that euphoric feeling was better than Pop ever felt. While he sat there stuck, Julio and Paquito just cracked up laughing. ***"It's good ?!?!"*** Paquito said. This was by far the purest cocaine that my dad ever came in contact with. He was more than satisfied so he didn't hesitate in giving Julio the rest of the money.

That was the day my dad began his journey to being the biggest coke dealer in the area. No one was murdered. No one was robbed. It was merely a business deal between my dad and a Cuban; the beginning of a flourishing business relationship that would last for years...

Uncle Ty and my dad quickly became ' The Connect' for a majority of hustlers around, either directly or indirectly. They never stopped hustling hand-to-hand to individual fiends. That was normalcy through the years. If you came down Red Bug wanting a kilo of cocaine, you could get that. If you came looking for a $20 rock, you could get that. Julio kept the kilos coming. My dad and Uncle Ty were buying ten to fifteen kilos a month back then, DuPont didn't stand a chance. Pop finally quit a little while after he connected with Julio. He was making more money in a day than most of his coworkers were making in a month.

Now of course, my sister and I didn't want for anything. We always wore the latest fashions, had the hottest shoes, and basically had anything a child would want at that time. All the kids in the neighborhood loved to come over. We were the first in the neighborhood to have satellite television, a Nintendo; we had the latest and greatest. Most evenings when I had my friends over, my mom would pack all of us in the car and take us to McDonald's. A lot of times, my friends who rode with us didn't have money. That didn't matter; my mom would always buy for everybody. Most of the parents in the community made a helluva lot less money than my dad.

CHAPTER 4 – SHE GAVE ME 'NORMAL'

As my dad's cocaine enterprise grew, things got worse between him and my mom. He didn't have a job he had to be at, so nothing was holding him back from going out of town more frequently. If he was home, he was hustling and really didn't spend a whole lot of family time. That was how things always were, but I guess my mom thought things would change after he stopped working at DuPont.

Pop and Uncle Ty started going to the beach a whole lot more. My cousins at the beach were making major moves. Pop was turning a few kilos a week right there in Hallsboro, but our cousins were selling a whole lot more down at the beach. Uncle Ty had a room at my grandparents, an apartment in Hallsboro, but he also had an apartment at the beach. Sometimes my dad wouldn't come home for a few days, and most of those times, he was down at the beach with his cousins and Uncle Ty. They had their little crew selling in Hallsboro, and they were going down to the beach making moves.

Julio and Paquito were driving all the way up from Miami to Hallsboro almost every two weeks. It was the same thing every time. They would pull to the back of the house, sit there and pull the dashboard out of the van to get the kilos out of the stash compartment, and Big Mike would give them their money and they would leave. Other times, Pop wouldn't even be home when they came. I remember a lot of nights that they would show up when he wasn't there, and they would just go to sleep in the van until he showed up; sometimes Big Mike wouldn't show up until the next morning.

One day when they came Pop wasn't home and they waited around for a while. I was home when they got there, but I left walking up the street to go play basketball at the park. I figured my dad was going to come in a little while, but when I got back home, they were still waiting. As I walked up the driveway Paquito and Julio got out. They usually spoke to me when they came, but they almost always just stayed in the van and just rolled down the window to speak. My mom and sister weren't home, but they never really interacted with them anyway. Mama honestly didn't like anybody who did business with Mike, but she tolerated them for the sake of staying out of my Pop's business.

Paquito always tried to make small talk with me about sports because every time he saw me I was either playing in the yard or walking with my basketball, football, or baseball glove. Neither one of them looked like they were trying to make small talk right then. They were looking pretty serious.

"Hey Petey, can you put something in the house for Mike for me?" Paquito said. His Cuban accent was pretty cool to me because it resembled how Tony and Manny talked in the movie Scarface. I told him yea and he reached in the van and handed me a big black gym bag.

"Put this inside where nobody will see it, and make sure Mike gets it" Paquito said. The whole time Julio was looking around to make sure nobody was passing by or looking. *"Don't look inside the bag Petey. This is something very important for your daddy. Go on, run inside and put it up. Tell Mike we'll call him later"* Paquito said. It was a little heavy, but I managed to run it inside to my father's closet. Now you know I looked in that bag as soon as I got inside. That was the most drugs I'd ever seen in my life at that point. There was ten kilos of coke in there. When I came back outside, my mom and my sister were pulling up. Julio and Paquito had already gotten back in the van and had moved it onto the grass so my mom could make it through the driveway to where she normally parked.

She didn't look happy that they were there, and when she got out of the car, she screamed at me to go back inside. She gave one of those hello waves without looking at them; you know the wave you give somebody when you really don't care for them too much.

I think Paquito and Julio may have stayed out there for a few more minutes before they finally just left. Later when I heard my dad pulling up when he got home, I met him outside and told him. He didn't waste any time at all. He went inside to get the bag, and left with it. My dad kept some drugs at the house, but large quantities like that always went to one of his stash spots around Hallsboro.

When McGruff the Crime Dog use to come to our school, he showed us pictures of what drugs looked like and told us to "Just Say No", but he never showed us what a kilo of cocaine looked like. I guess they didn't think kids my age would ever see anything like that, especially in a small town like Hallsboro.

During those days, you could find me at either one of four places most of the time; my house, my grandparent's house, the park, or my cousin Birdie's. Birdie lived down this dirt road almost right on the other side of my grandparent's house. He was almost two years older than me and my friends but he spent a lot of time with us. We kind of looked up to him because he was always showing us how to play a sport, go fishing or anything outdoorsy. He was like the O.G of our little crew.

Birdie always had a few big dogs like Labrador Retrievers and German Sheppard's, and every single one of them were trained to the T. A lot of times we hung out there to play with the dogs or play football outside. He stayed with his grandmother, Mrs. Mary Powell, and her son Lee, AKA' Dog'. Mrs. Mary married a guy from a different set of Powell's; no relation to us. Years later, we found out that 'Dog' was actually very closely related to us. We'll get to exactly how in a second. That's the big family secret my grandparents kept for years.

When my homeboys and I would go to Birdie's his Uncle Lee would always kick it with us. He was about 17-years-old at the time and drove a school bus for Hallsboro High School. He was still a student there, but back in them days they allowed licensed students to drive school buses and go to school to. That bus was always parked in the yard, and sometimes Dog would let us help him wash it. He was cool as a fan and always dressed to the 9's.

Him and my cousin Ann, who stayed with my grandparents, were close friends and hung out a lot. Dog would come over to see Ann sometimes, and I would catch a ride with him to go to the Hallsboro football and basketball games. I caught a ride with Ann sometimes, but for the most part I would ride with Dog. Most nights after a game was over we would all go to the McDonald's in Whiteville. That was the hot spot after the games back then. The whole parking lot would be full of high school kids just hanging out. Of course a lot of fights happened there, but that didn't stop people from going, it was tradition. After a few hours most of the kids went home because they had curfews. The kids who didn't have curfews went straight to the Odyssey Club downtown Whiteville.

The parking lot was the place to be for everybody who was too young to go inside. We would always meet up with Ann there.

Ann and Dog got stuck dragging me around with them all the time. My grandmother didn't mind, as long as I was with one of them. I was hanging out with them till about 2 o'clock in the morning before I even became a teenager. By the time I was twelve, I was already hanging out, drinking and smoking. Dog became one of my best friends, and he was seven years older than me. I always wondered why Grandma would let me hang out that late with Dog. Years later, it all made sense...

My family was outgrowing our house, and Pop knew we needed more space. I think he may have started looking for houses here and there over a course of time, but never made a move on anything. But one day the perfect situation presented itself. There was an old man that lived right up the street named Mr. Elliot. I'm not too sure exactly how old he was, but he was definitely old enough to be my great grandfather. He had hooked up with a lady who was a lot younger than he was in Hallsboro and she rocked his world. I forget her name, but she had Mr. Elliot's nose wide open. That was the talk of the town. Well somehow she talked Mr. Elliot into moving in with her, and he did what any sugar daddy would have done to keep that pretty young thang; he moved in. While everybody else around the way was laughing at the fact that his nose was wide open, my dad was in Mr. Elliot's ear about buying his house. One thing about Big Mike that everybody knew is that he got what he wanted. After he met with Mr. Elliot a few times, he came home to tell us we were moving. The house was less than a mile up the street from my grandparents, and it was a whole lot bigger than what we were staying in. The day he told us that we were moving, that was one of them days that I saw my mother's heart smile. They stood in the kitchen and kissed for what seemed like forever after he gave us the news.

The new house was 3 bedrooms, but it was a whole lot more spacious. Each room had walk-in closets; the den and living room were enormous. We had more than enough room for our family and it gave us a fresh start. My mom was happier than she'd been in a long time. Me and my sister loved everything about that house, especially how big our new rooms were. My dad even started staying home a lot more - for a little while at least. The new house had a real nice closed-in porch in the back. That's where Pop would spend most of his time when he was home. One thing that was always certain-After Spike got off work, he was coming straight over to the house to drink, smoke weed, and joke with my dad all night while pop hustled. Uncle Ty would come over a lot and a few of his other partners around the way. Most of the people who would come back there were coming to buy drugs. A few would chill for a while, but for the most part, Pop would serve them and they would leave.

When the word got around that we'd moved into the new spot, the traffic started coming. At first it wasn't that bad, nothing out of the ordinary, but then a whole lot of new faces started coming around; a lot more traffic. I guess since Big Mike purchased a new crib, everybody knew he was really getting to some money. That's generally how things work in life; everybody wants to be associated with what they consider to be successful. Everybody in the street wanted to be around Big Mike, especially the hustlers. I figure they wanted to see exactly how he and my Uncle Ty were making that much money.

My grandma Alma would come by the new house a lot, pretty much every day, which wasn't a surprise being that I was her favorite grandchild and we lived so close. Her and my mom would talk for hours when she visited, mostly about my dad. Grandma had faith in my parent's relationship, that kind of faith that could only come from a woman that's held her marriage intact for many years. She gave my mom a whole lot of counseling to cope with things. For the most part it helped, but there would still be times that my mom just couldn't take it. I loved seeing grandma pull up in the yard. Her heart was golden-I felt it every time she was near. In my heart-of-hearts I'm almost sure my mother would have divorced my father early on if it wasn't for my grandma.

The older I got, the clearer it became as to why my mom stayed so stressed out with my dad. Everybody has different things that they can deal with. Some women probably would have left the moment my dad started selling drugs. Some women might have left when he started hanging out all night and not coming home for extended periods of time. My mom's biggest issue with him was the women. It was bad enough that women would see him out in public and want to sit there and have long conversations about nothing. It was even worse that most of all those women wanted him and they didn't care one bit that he was married. You can't control who comes on to you, the only person that you can control is you. That was my dad's problem; he couldn't control himself. The more money he made, the worse it got. I grew up watching my mom love him through all that hurt.

I didn't start getting into girls until I was teenager. My first love stole my heart when I was in the 8th grade. Her name was Dawana, and to this day, she's one of the sweetest spirits I've ever met. My cousin Mario was dating her cousin and I guess they were trying to play matchmaker because they thought they were the cutest couple at school. It all started with a phone call.

Mario came to my house one Friday after school and was all hyped up about hooking me up with Dawana. He tried his best to get me to figure out who she was, but I really couldn't because she was two years younger than me. I never really paid any attention to the younger girls at school.

After he wasted all that time trying to get me to figure out exactly who she was, I asked him the only thing that mattered to any twelve-year-old boy at that time. *"Man, is she fine?"* When he told me she was a pretty red bone, that's all I needed to hear. Dawana was spending that weekend at Mario's girlfriend's house. He called his girlfriend from my house and they put me and Dawana on the phone with each other. He'd already told me that she was shy, and when I got on the phone she hardly said a word. She was shy just like he told me, but she wasn't shy enough to ask me whether or not I was ugly. I just laughed at her when she asked me that. That night we were all going to hook up at the basketball game. Here I was, twelve-years-old going on my first blind date.

That night Dog picked me and Mario up. When we told him that I was going to meet up with a girl that night, he gave me pure hell. He asked Mario a million and one questions about her, and kept asking me *"Pete you ready? If you scared just say you scared."* Mario laughed the whole way to the school, and I was just sitting there trying to hold my composure because to be totally honest, I was nervous. Dog wasn't making it no better talking my head off about what to do.

"Pete, when you walk in the gym you gotta go in there stepping like you own the whole damn building. If she know that you nervous, she goin' clown you now. Bump what everybody else in there doing, keep all your attention on her; look her right in the eyes the whole time. If that chic ugly, be nice to her tonight then just don't call her no more..." He just kept going on-and-on. I think he was trying to be funny, and it worked because Mario was laughing his ass off in the backseat. I just sat there trying my best to be cool and not show them exactly how nervous I was.

Me and Dog always made a grand entrance in the gym when we went to the games. Big Mike and my mom made sure I had the freshest clothes, and Dog had a job so he always had money to buy nice fits. Mario has always been a bigger guy, but always had the confidence of a pit bull in a cat fight. We walked into that gym that night like we were walking the red carpet; all eyes were on us.

Didn't take long for us to spot Mario's girlfriend in the bleachers. As soon as we saw her, right beside her sat the girl who would end up capturing my heart for years to come; Dawana. They were about mid-court half-way up the bleachers. I couldn't take my eyes off her, mainly because I wanted to make sure she was as cute as Mario made her out to be.

When we first sat down, I didn't really think she was feeling me at all. It was just the fact that she was really shy. I spent most of that game talking her ear off while she just sat there and smiled. She was an innocent girl, raised in a single-parent household by her mom and was one of the smartest girls in her class. Someone had already told her that I had a little attitude, really didn't make good grades and my family wasn't exactly the Huxtables. She didn't care; she just kept complimenting me on my smile. Have her tell it, I had the prettiest teeth in America. Long-story short, we hit it off that night and ended up being boyfriend and girlfriend that next day. You know how puppy love goes...Years later when federal agents came for me, they picked her up too. Sweet really didn't matter.

I was becoming a little man during those years, really developing character. My attitude got a whole lot better around then. I still cut up at school, but it was mostly just clowning around, not nearly as bad as I was in my early years. I was an all-around all-star in sports. Between Mike Mobley on the court or field and Uncle Ty off the field, I had the best coaching a young athlete could have. My girlfriend was one of the prettiest-smartest girls at school, but there was one thing that separated me from every other young man in school. The men in my family were kingpins. They didn't just sell a lot, they sold the most. Most of the kids I knew would have loved to be in my shoes, but they were just on the outside looking in. They didn't know that almost every few days I would come home and catch my mom crying her heart out. They didn't see that all those years of crying wouldn't mend her broken heart. They didn't know what it was like to know in your heart that your father loves you, but often feel like he was millions of miles away. They didn't feel what I felt, like when my father would be out of town for weeks or even months at a time, never hearing his voice or even have a remote clue as to where he was at. Yea, the clothes were nice, the money was nice, but the kids who may have thought about trading places with me had no idea what it was like to feel what I felt and see what I saw.

My relationship with my grandmother matured. I was still her baby, but we talked about everything that was going on in my life; the good, the bad and the ugly. Like I told you, my grandpa would go through these phases that he would eat the same thing every day for years. During this time, he was stuck on stew beef. After school sometimes I would go over their house and spend some time with them. Usually I would get on the phone with Dawana for a while and talk until my grandmother called me and Ann to the kitchen table for dinner. When we sat down to eat, she was still standing in front of the stove cooking grandpa's stew beef. Ann and grandma would always pick on me about having Dawana, and I couldn't do anything but smile.

"Grandma Alma, Petey was in there telling that girl he wanted to kiss her on the phone a little while ago." Ann said while she smirked and glanced over at me. My grandma would never take things like that too seriously. She would just turn and look at me to see what kind of expression I had on my face. Usually I would be looking at Ann across the table with my jaw dropped because she'd told my business.

"Baby you gotta treat that girl right. If you don't get them school grades up she ain't goin' want you after a while. Don't no woman want no dummy. That girl got her stuff together and she just as pretty as she can be. And don't be thinking bout no kissing yet. If you bring a baby home, how you goin' take care of it?" Grandma would say the realest things in the sweetest voice. You had no other choice but to take her seriously.

Uncle Ty ended up buying a little shop in the neighborhood. It had been around for years, and the owner was just getting tired of it I think. It was almost directly in front of my grandparent's house down this little dirt road. A church always sat on the main road. The shop was a little ways behind it off the road. It was a small wooden building, about the size of a double-wide trailer. It had a tin roof, but it was pretty nice inside. There was a pool table in there, a small dance floor, a Pac Man and Galaga video game, a juke box, and a private room that only a few people were allowed in. There was a nice couch and a television in there. That's where Unc sold a lot of big drugs. That's also were a lot of the men close to us took their side women; if they were allowed to go back there.

Uncle Ty sold a lot of things at the shop; all kinds of candy, sodas, pickled eggs, liquor, beer, and of course – all the drugs your money could buy. Very quickly it became one of the neighborhood hangouts when Uncle Ty bought it. Around this time Spike had quit working at DuPont and was already hanging around every day, so Uncle Ty just let him run the shop. Having Spike there was all strategy. Spike kept people in there laughing, having a good time, and spending money. The other good thing was that my dad would come down there every night and hangout with Spike. Wherever my dad went, he was 'big timing'; buying drinks for everybody. With him coming through there, it was like a party up there every night. Between the shop, the park, the liquor houses, and our house, Red Bug Rd was netting the 'Powell Boys' well over a million dollars a year right in the small community of Hallsboro in the mid-80's.

Most nights, my friends and I hung out at the shop playing pool or arcade games. Most of them had to go home when it got dark. As for me, I stayed out till either Uncle Ty or my Dad went home. Sometimes Dog would come up there and I would catch a ride with him. A lot of times Dog would stop by and scoop me up if he was going somewhere like the mall or somewhere like that. More than likely if you saw Dog's tan Ford Festiva somewhere, I was in the passenger seat. Some days we rode all day. You could put ten dollar's worth of gas in the tank and ride all week.

CHAPTER 5 – UNLAWFUL ENTREPRENEURSHIP

Me and Dawana would see each other every day in school. A lot of older people, especially her mom, couldn't believe that a nice, young, innocent girl like her would date a young man like me. I had a little attitude, my dad and uncle did what they did and I wasn't really focused on my grades, but I was a good kid; very respectable. That's the thing that won all of my teachers over and the older people in the community. Ultimately, that's why Dawana's mom didn't have a big problem with me-well, not until later on.

Hanging out at Uncle Ty's shop was the thing to do after school during that time. Everybody who was anybody in the community would stop by on a daily basis, even if they only stopped by to shoot the breeze for a few. There were drugs being sold there but it wasn't like you're probably thinking. Preachers, teachers, grandmother's; those types of people came there every day. When you came in you were treated with southern hospitality; it was a business. The only thing that was different was the fact that you could buy drugs there. Pop knew about Dawana and that I was getting into girls. Uncle Ty, my dad and Spike would always pick with me. Pop would be in there having a few drinks with everybody at night and look over at me and say things like ***"Man, you ain't getting no butt yet is*** *you?"* Of course I would lie because I wanted to look cool in front of everybody, but Pop knew I was still a virgin. Uncle Ty would always jokingly say things to make me comfortable when my dad got on me. *"Mike, the boys say Petey done smashed all the baddest broads in school. Them girls can't keep they hands off of 'em. He got Dog taking him to they house when they mamas ain't home."* Then he would look at me and say something like *"Pete I done heard bout ya. You a tough man."* Everybody knew Uncle Ty was lying, but it made the situation a whole lot more comfortable. Every boy goes through that phase were people start questioning whether or not they're having sex yet. Those were some funny times. Every now and then Pop would get on me bad. He was always joking, but every boy gets a little uncomfortable when that happens.

...And then one night it happened. A whole bunch of people were in the shop one night drinking and shooting the breeze while the jukebox was blasting. It was kind of late, so all my homeboys had already gone home for the night. I was the only person in there my age. That's when Ms. Diane came in.

Ms. Diane, till this day, is still one of the most beautiful women I've ever laid eyes on in my entire life. When I say that, I'm not exaggerating the least bit. She had a caramel skin tone, no stomach, a small frame, but her butt... it was humungous and perfectly round.

As far as how she looked, she put you in the mindset of the lady that was in that Michael Jackson 'Thriller' video; Ola Ray. When she walked pass the park when me and my homeboys would be out there playing basketball, or walked pass when we were outside, we couldn't help it; we all would just sit there and stare for as long as we could. It wasn't just us looking; it was all the men around-she was just that bad.

But when she came into the shop that night, she had already been drinking a little bit and started dancing as soon as she hit the door. Pop saw how I was looking at her and leaned over and whispered something to Uncle Ty. It was a few other women in there that night, but none of them looked half as good as she did. It seemed like the party turned up another level when she came in.

She walked around to speak to everybody, smiling like she always did, and when she got to Pop, he pulled her to the side to talk to her. I stayed out of grown folk business, so I really didn't pay close attention to see what they were talking about. A few moments later, my dad called for me to come with him. He was walking towards the private room. I'd been in there before to watch TV, but this was sorta like a presidential escort. I didn't know what was about to happen. As soon as we stepped inside the room, Diane was coming in right behind us. That's when I got nervous as hell. My dad didn't even close the door behind her when she stepped in. He said, ***"Take care of my son"*** and closed the door behind him when he walked out. I was nervous, didn't know what was going on, but I wasn't about to let this beautiful woman see it.

Ms. Diane was in her mid-twenties at the time, and here I was thirteen-years-old. She always used to tell me how good I looked when she saw me out and about, but I would have never expected to end up in a one-on-one situation with her; not in a million years. I was so nervous when I first walked in with my dad, and everything was happening so quick, that I didn't notice that there was a porno playing on the television until my dad walked out-the volume was turned all the way down. She just stood in front of me with her beautiful self and grabbed my hand. She walked me over to the couch that was in there and sat down right in front of me. Her sex appeal was out of this world, and the fact that she was tipsy just enhanced it.

"Petey you ain't no little boy no more baby. Pull them pants down." She said. As nervous as I was, I wasn't about to show it. The only thing I could do at that moment was pull down my pants. As soon as I did, she went to work. My eyes rolled up in the back of my head and I felt like I was in Heaven for two whole minutes. That night, I stepped into manhood; at least that's how I felt. I never knew she was smoking crack until that night. I think my dad may have given her ten dollar's worth of rock for servicing me. I saw her in that private room every few days after that. Don't judge me, I'm human. Smh.

My hormones were in full gear after then. Dawana was a good girl. It took me forever to even kiss her. Sex or anything concerning sex was the last thing on her mind. As for me, I couldn't wait on her. I was chasing skirts like dogs chase cats, and when I was in the ninth grade, I had the perfect bachelor pad to entertain the girls I was chasing. Dog rented a house down a little dirt road right beside my grandmother's. My cousin Dre and I would hang out there a lot. Dog was working a construction gig then with a guy named John Junious, everybody called him Moe. Moe owned a local construction company, John Junious Construction. Moe had Dog working hard, but he paid him well.

Spike also worked with them from time to time. To be honest, Spike really didn't have to work; Uncle Ty and my Dad made sure he always had money. Everyone there knew Spike and my Pop were tight so they would always chat about Big Mike at work.

Dre was two years older than me. He was actually Dog's nephew, Dog's brother; Joe's son. Joe was in prison at the time for murdering a white couple years earlier. I think Joe was dating their daughter and they had an issue with it. Like I said, I don't really know exactly what happened, but they ended up being murdered by him. Moving right along, Joe was Dre's father and Dog's nephew, so he would spend a lot of time at Dog's spot. Dre was a live wire, always liked to fight. He went to school off and on, but he was ultimately a good dude.

We would have different girls in and out of that house every week. Sometimes they would find a way over; sometimes when Dog got off work he would go pick them up. However they got there, we were entertaining them when they came; drinking, watching movies, and smoking weed. I wasn't smoking then, but everybody else was. I lost my virginity in that house and after I lost it, I just kept going and going. Dawana and I didn't break up. She had no idea what I was doing. As far as she was concerned, I was her 'Mr. Right 'and I could do no wrong. If she would have found out about what I was doing, that would have been the imminent end of a beautiful thing.

Big Mike and Uncle Ty were doing their thing. Julio and Paquito were coming on schedule and the traffic coming through Red bug kept on growing. Big Mike kept going out of town meeting new connects and hustling. Uncle Ty stayed back and forth from the beach to Hallsboro doing the same thing. Spike would hold down the shop when Uncle Ty went out town, and my dad and Uncle Ty's crew would hold down the drugs. The business was booming, and in those days, the late 80's, the demand was up.

Pop never really liked hustling on the back porch of our home and felt like he needed a spot to hustle and chill. Some nights it got loud out there, and Big Mike really didn't like all the noise so close to the house. He decided on building a spot right behind the house. Big Mike, with his bigger than life personality that everybody loved, decided on building a three story building right behind us; the infamous barn.

The barn didn't take a lot a long time at all to go up. Normally, a project like the barn took about six months to complete back then. Big Mike's money got it done in three months. The barn was the new spectacle of the neighborhood. Pop loved it, and built it with the intention of it being the hottest dope spot in Hallsboro. You could come there to workout, chill out and buy all the dope you wanted; that's exactly what people did and I do mean A LOT OF PEOPLE. My mom hated it. She was up to her wits end with my dad's mess and was just getting tired of it all. I watched her heart hurt more and more.

My crew pretty much ran the high school then. We were only ninth graders at the time, but we were all star athletes and the most popular dudes on campus...

There was 'Ant'. Everybody knows him as Rooster, big heart, the type of guy that would help anybody; real compassionate. Ant was a monster on the baseball field-ended up signing a pro contract. Rooster's mom had four other children and his step dad lived with them. His step dad used to beat on Rooster's mom, it's rumored that he murdered someone before. He and Rooster would get into it all the time. One day after things got crazy between them, his step father shot at him. That was the last straw. Big Mike let Rooster come live with us until we graduated high school.

There was 'Juice'. Juice came down from D.C to stay with his grandmother; he was getting out of hand up there. Juice brought an edge to the crew. He was a slick dude, funny than a mug and liked them girls.

My man Tim was with us. Tim was all around 'good people'. He ended up being one of my most loyal friends through the years; also ended up doing a federal bid too. Then we had Kendall. Real cool guy. Kendall was a hard working young man and a respectable person.

If you saw one of us, you saw all of us. As always, I had the freshest clothes on campus. I always had a little money in my pocket, was pretty much one of the best athletes in the county, everybody knew my family and the girls were in love with me. I was making my rounds through them, but only one had my heart; Dawana.

We would hang out on the handicap ramp that led into the lunchroom at school. We were in the same homeroom and most of us had the same classes. Mike Mobley ended up being a teacher at the high school. Mr. Mobley was a coach and he taught consumer math. He wanted to yank all of us up from junior varsity to varsity in every sport.

During that year, Dog actually got one of my classmates pregnant. He was seven years older than her but his mom and her mom sat down and made an agreement to make sure they would come together and take good care of the child. Dog was a hardworking man and always made good on that promise. That same year, his brother Joe got out of prison. When Joe came around, everything started changing quickly.

With news of a baby on the way, Dog felt like he had to make more money. Somehow, the temptation to do dirt became too much for him. There was so much money being made on Red Bug, he figured he could get in on the action as well, and that's exactly what he did.

Dog was like family, so when he went to Uncle Ty and told him that he wanted to hustle, Unc didn't bat an eye; he fronted him crack to sell. It wasn't much, maybe an ounce. It was just enough to pay Uncle Ty back and put a little over a thousand dollars in his pocket. Selling it wasn't hard at all. There was more than enough traffic on Red Bug and Dog already knew most of the crack fiends in Hallsboro. It took him a few days to figure out what he was doing, it ain't rocket science, but after then he was making more money than he'd ever made in his life. After a few weeks of that he gave Moe his resignation and became a full-time hustler.

After school, when I didn't have practice, I rarely went straight home. It was usually to my grandparents to grab a bite to eat and call Dawana, then to the shop with my dudes, or Dog's crib. Dog's crib was slowly turning into a 24/hr a day trap spot (drug house). It really didn't matter because I'd been accustomed to being around drugs my entire life; plus Dog always had women over there. If one came to see him, he would get one of them to bring a friend or two over for me and Dre.

As soon as Joe got out of prison, the red carpet was rolled out for him. My dad and Uncle Ty immediately put some money in his pocket and bought him clothes. They always looked out for people in the community. They paid lights bills if families didn't have money, bought kids school clothes, etc. Dog also made sure Joe had a few dollars. Joe couldn't believe how much money Dog was making. When he saw how Uncle Ty and Big Mike were putting their hustle down, his mind was literally blown. Dog was giving him dope to sell, as well as my dad and Uncle Ty. He started making a little money, but he wasn't really a hustler. The whole time this was happening, he and Dre were pretty much getting to know each other. They were slowly figuring each other out. Joe stayed with his and Dog's mom, Mrs. Mary.

Right after Joe came home, Dog decided to move into a bigger place. The place he chose was a trailer right off of Red Bug, a little ways down from my dad's house. A couple, James and Sharon White, had been living there for years but decided to move and rent the place out. It was a nice single wide trailer, nothing too much, but definitely an upgrade. James White and Uncle Ty were really close. For a long time they would be with each other every day. James was a great handyman, the guy could fix anything. Uncle Ty built a home right beside my grandparents, opposite the side our old house was, and needed James around to help him with a lot of the work. Over a course of time they developed a close friendship. Uncle Ty really took it hard when James was murdered years later.

A guy claims that James was trying to break into his house, so he shot and killed him. Word on the street is the guy owed James money for some handy work he did for him, and they got into a heated argument when James went to him looking for his pay. Either way it went, the guy didn't get charged with anything.

When Dog moved into the trailer, his house became the new hangout for my whole crew. We could drink, smoke, bring all the girls we wanted to-it was the perfect bachelor pad, and Dog loved us being there. We partied our asses off when Dog first got there, but he never let us get too out of hand, he had rules.

Regardless of how late we stayed up and partied, we had to go to school the next day. He may have been a drug dealer, but he knew how important school was and wanted us to value it to. We cooked and ate like kings over there, but before we all either left or went to sleep, he designated somebody to wash the dishes and take the trash out. We basically did what we wanted to, but we had to respect that man's house; he treated us like grown men and expected us to act like such.

Throughout the ninth grade, we spent most of our time there. A few more guys from the neighborhood started hanging out over there too when they heard about girls from all over the county coming through on a regular basis, and all the partying we were doing.

One of those guys was my cousin Scott. Most people know him as 'Skeeter Rock.' Skeeter Rock was light-skinned and real short. This dude was the comedian of the crew, and if his skinny self could, he would have spent every night in the club dancing; super party animal.

The other guy was Mark. Most of his life people called him 'Killer', because he really looked like one. Killer was bald-headed and cut up like a professional wrestler. He would fight anyone, he didn't care who you were-he didn't even care whether or not you had a gun. The surprising thing about him was that he was a funny dude. He and Skeeter Rock would go back and forth joking on each other 24-7.

Dog stayed on the move and the traffic never stopped, so when we would be there and he left, he would always leave us some dope to serve the fiends that came. He trusted me more than he trusted the rest of them, but he would leave crack and coke for Dre to sell during that time. That was how Dre kept a few dollars in his pock-et. I told you Dre was the live wire. He was the first one in our crew, our age, to start hustling.

CHAPTER 6 – NOTHING LIKE FAMILY
THE SECRET

The day the big family secret came out...

Joe started coming around to the trailer a lot when Dog moved in. He was cool as a fan, and always straight to the point. One night we were all there chilling and Dog left for a little while. He was gone to pick up some more coke from my dad or Uncle Ty. At any rate, as soon as Dog got back he went straight to the stove to cook the cocaine he had just picked up into crack. I'd seen my dad and Unc do it a million times, but everybody in the crew was always fascinated by it in those days so they always stood around and stared at Dog when he cooked. A few moments after he got going someone was banging on the door. Skeeter Rock walked over to check out who it was. ***"Ain't nobody but yo' worrisome ass daddy Dre"*** he said, as sarcastically as knew how. The police never came around, but everybody in the house was always paranoid when Dog got a package.

When Joe walked in, he spoke to everybody like he always did, and walked into the kitchen with Dog. We all went back into the living room, but Joe was talking loud enough for all of us to hear what he was saying.

"Man how much Ty sell you that for" Joe said. That's what he assumed, but that particular time my Dad had sold it to him. Dog replied *"Why you all in my business? I ain't even get this from Ty."* Dog wasn't really trying to have a whole lot of conversation at the time; he was busy trying to cook up his dope.

"Dog, they ain't even looking out for you bruh. Your own brothers, flesh and damn blood, cutting ya damn throat." Joe said.

When he said that, everybody in the room head turned towards the kitchen. You could have heard a flea fart it was so quiet. Suddenly Joe noticed that everybody was looking like they were, his neck snapped back towards Dog and his voice raised a whole lot more.

"Bruh you mean to tell me ain't nobody told you? Dog...you know you ain't like me and Dre'; we crazy as hell! You all laid back and calm! Boy, Ty and Mike is yo damn brothers. Emory-Powell-is-your-daddy!!!"

When Joe said it, he was just standing there staring at Dog in amazement. Me and the rest of the boys didn't know what to say, but we knew by the way Joe was saying it, that he wasn't playing at all.

"Petey, you mean to tell me you been around this fool all this time and you ain't know this yo' uncle?!?! Ya'll ain't gotta believe me. Let's go to the shop right now!!! Ty down there, I just walked from down that way."

Dog didn't know what to say, nor did anybody else in that room. While we were sitting there quiet, Joe just kept going on and on about how he couldn't believe that we didn't know. As soon as Dog finished cooking his package, we all packed up in Dog and Skeeter Rock's cars and went straight to the shop.

When we pulled up, we all hopped out those cars as quick as we could and rushed inside. There weren't too many people there but Big Mike and Uncle Ty were inside; that's all that mattered. When we got inside they thought something was wrong. Both of their eyes got big as silver dollars.

Joe walked right up to Uncle Ty and Big Mike and asked could he speak to them in private. They both got up and walked towards the private room. Joe walked right behind them and looked at Dog and signaled for him to come along. They stayed in that room for a long time. Me and the rest of the boys just stood around quiet. The other few folks in there didn't know what was going on, but there was a nervous tension in the air.

See, we'd heard rumors through the years that my grandfather used to cheat on my grandmother but no one ever took it too seriously. You know how people in small communities always start rumors because they don't have anything else better to do with their time. When they walked out of that room, they all had pleasant looks on their faces. That's the moment I realized that all of those rumors were true. When Uncle Ty walked pass me, he looked me in my eyes and shook his head. ***"Yea Pete, that's your Uncle."*** He said, as he kept walking to go back to the bar stool he was sitting at when we came in.

Me, Ty, my dad, Joe, and Dog walked over to my grandparents' house a few minutes after they came out of there, it was right across the street. My grandfather wasn't home at the time, but they sat Grandma Alma down and told her what had just happened.

"Well, that was Emory's job to tell y'all. That's exactly what a man is supposed to do..." my grandma said while she scanned everybody's eyes in the room. She was so sweet and poised at all times.

"I knew, but Emory was supposed to be the one to tell y'all. Me and Emory love each other, but this marriage ain't always been what everybody think. Nobody marriage is perfect. I'm glad y'all found out, but I just wish he would have told ya' before now."

Grandma stood up, walked towards Dog, and hugged him with one of those tight hugs grandmas give their grandchildren when they're proud of them. They sat in there and talked for a little while before we all went back to the shop.

After that night, the bond I already had with Dog grew a whole lot stronger. Everything started making sense. That's why my grandmother never had an issue with me being out with Dog when I was so young. That was the reason me and him got along so well, even though we were seven years apart. During all those years, we didn't have a clue. It doesn't take a rocket scientist to figure out how Dog's relationship with Big Mike and Ty went after the secret was out.

Right before we found out about Dog being my uncle, he was buying two or three ounces of coke from Pop and Uncle Ty every time he would re-up. Well, the very next day, my dad gave Dog a quarter kilo; (nine ounces-street value=$14k-$18k). Dog went from being a around-the-way hustler to playing with the big boys over-night. From that day forward, Dog was one of the 'Powell Boys'. The traffic at Dog's house grew because he could give the fiends that were already coming more weight, and now he could sell the small time hustlers in the area packages. There was so much traffic down Red Bug at the time; Dog could make a couple grand a day off Big Mike and Uncle Ty's excess.

Dawana was my heart. Spending time with her at school, on the phone, whenever we would get together was priceless. I cherished every moment. Regardless of what was going on in my life at the time, she brought normalcy. I made a serious effort to keep her away from everything that was going on in my life, and for years I did an incredible job. I was sleeping with a lot of girls all over; even girls who went to school with us-she didn't have a clue. No one could have taken me away from her, not even the grown women I was messing with who had money, cars, etc. She owned my heart, and that wasn't a secret. Pop had a few cars, but one of his most prized possessions at the time was his Jag. It was a 4-door metallic blue Jag with peanut butter interior and a V12 engine. Most times when he went out of town, that's what he would drive. I wouldn't be lying if I said it was the nicest car in the community. My dad had this air about him that gave him this successful aura. He made everybody feel like somebody, regardless of who they were. He respected his customers. He was a hustler's hustler, but more so than that, he was genuinely a good man; he just sold cocaine.

I remember him always telling Julio and Paquito to never to go into town when they came around. He was referring to the city of Whiteville, which bordered Hallsboro to the west. Whiteville is the county seat of Columbus County and was always flooded with city cops and sheriff patrols. The risk was just too high to go into Whiteville.

Every now and then they wouldn't listen. They would hop off the highway to go to McDonald's or one of the stores in town.

When they did, pop would always make a big deal out of it and lecture them for a few. Big Mike had a good thing going with those guys, and like anyone else, he wanted to protect his business.

They didn't listen. For one, they had a whole lot more money than my dad; they were his connect. For two, they'd been selling cocaine for so long that they'd grown arrogant, you know; thought they knew everything.

A new shopping center was being built right off of 701 in Whiteville. Got no clue why they decided to go in town in the first place, and really don't have a clue why they decided to park their van on the building site and fall asleep that night, but they did. Somehow a city cop rolled up on them while they were sleeping. That old van was in no condition for them to lead the police on a high speed chase. For whatever reason it was, they ended up getting arrested. Maybe it was for the gun Paquito always had, who knows, but when the van was impounded, the police found it all; twenty kilos of cocaine.

My dad and Uncle Ty didn't find out what happened until they watched the news the following day. That wasn't the end of it. While they were being transported to court by sheriff deputies, Paquito managed to escape. Heaven only knows how much time Julio got. We never heard from either one of them again. One thing that's for certain, they didn't rat on my dad or Ty. They were standup guys.

In the business of cocaine, people get caught, killed, and disappear all the time. That's one of those things that's never going to change; life happens. When it happens, it's not like the demand dies. It's certainly not like the supply is affected in any way. As long as plants can grow, there will always be a market for cocaine.

My father didn't skip a beat. He hit the highway and went to get more coke. He had connects that he'd established relationships with from Chicago to New York, all the way down to Florida. Big Mike knew dope dealers everywhere so Julio and Paquito getting jammed up didn't mess up his flow. The only thing that was really affected was the convenience of having kilos delivered. Julio and Paquito getting jammed up just made him and Uncle Ty go harder.

My father always gave me a hard time when it came to money. It didn't matter that he was a millionaire; I couldn't ask him for lunch money without him giving me the third degree. I would be sitting there looking at him in amazement when he gave me flack about getting money from him. I couldn't stand it. Usually I would ask my mom for money when I needed it, but when she wasn't around, I had to go through hell-and-high water to get twenty or thirty dollars out of that man for stuff that I really needed. I guess he was teaching me how to be self-sufficient, but really, what was I supposed to do for cash then?

The thing that got to me was that it seemed like he treated everybody else better than me. He always looked out for people in the community, his crew, and his friends. My dad bought some of the guys in his crew cars, paid people's bills regularly, especially his women. I felt like he was just being hard on me for no reason.

My cousin Mont came to stay with us around that time. He was five years younger than me and my parents spoiled him. He was a great kid. Mont was extremely intelligent, respectable, and just like the rest of us in the family, he was an incredible athlete. Mont was my Aunt Karen's son, my mom's sister. He came to live with us when she was murdered.

When the crack epidemic hit, she got sucked in. When she realized that she had a problem, my parents immediately sent her to rehab. She was raising Mont in Whiteville and dating a guy from there for a few years before she went to rehab. When she made it through, all she wanted to do was have a fresh start. Her and Mont came to stay with us for a few weeks when she finished the program.

Aunt Karen was doing better and looking better than she had in years. She was optimistic about her new start and just happy that she was completely off drugs. Everybody was happy for her, it was a beautiful thing. She and Mont moved back into the house they were living in and things were going great. She quit dealing with a lot of the friends she had that were using, and was basically putting herself in a better position so she could continue making progress.

One night Mont called the house and begged me to come spend the night with him. I was his older cousin, so he looked up to me and thought I was the coolest guy on the planet. He begged me, but I had already made plans that night.

The guy my Aunt Karen had been with off-and-on for years came to their house that night. They got into a heated argument while little Mont was right there watching. Aunt Karen ended up running out of the front door and the guy ran out chasing right behind her. That was the last time Mont saw his mom alive. The asshole stabbed her to death right across the street behind a house. Mont was just a kid, and had to testify at the murder trial. A young child should never have to go through anything like that. He ended up staying with another one of my mom's sisters for a little while, and then my dad decided to move him in with us. My parents spoiled the hell out of him. I loved him and he became more than a cousin; that was my little brother.

With all the love Big Mike was showing Mont and everyone else, it honestly felt like he just hated the idea of giving me anything. I got tired of it. I know every parent wants to teach their sons self-sufficiency, but I was just a teenager in high school at the time. Between school, sports, the girls, and everything else I was doing; I didn't have time for a job bagging groceries or anything. **I did what the environment I was raised in showed me...**

CHAPTER 7 – FIRST BITE OF FORBIDDEN FRUIT

Uncle Ty would always give me pocket change. It wasn't a lot, maybe fifty to a hundred dollars a week, but it was enough to get me by during the week. As I got older, quite naturally I needed more money. Even more so than needing more money, I wanted my own.

I always felt like I could go to Unc and talk to him about anything, and honestly, I could. Well, all that frustration from my father giving me flack about asking him for money had built up, and I made it up in my mind that I was never going to ask him for anything again.

I caught up with Uncle Ty at his shop one day. I told him straight up that I needed my own. I explained everything to him about how frustrated I was with asking Pop for money all the time and him giving me the third degree. To make a long story short, I just came out and told him that I wanted to hustle. At first, he was upset.

"Petey what the hell you need money for? You keep a few dollars in your pocket! You ain't hurting for nothing. You living better than all the rest of the kids round here.

C'mon Pete, answer me son, what you need money for?!?! You got somebody pregnant?..." Uncle Ty was worked up, but I was so focused on not asking Big Mike for another dime that I didn't care.

"Unc, you know how Mike is. Every time I need something for school or anything, I got to hear his mouth. You ain't gotta keep giving me money, give me some weed or something and let me get it myself. If I don't get it from you, Imma find somebody to get it from-imma get it though..." I just had to be straight up with him because I was determined, one way or another, to get my hands on something.

For the next few days Unc' gave me the cold shoulder. I had already kind of figured that's what he was going to do; I knew he was upset with me. I didn't stop looking though. When I asked Dog, he told me no. I asked a few people in my dad's crew, they told me the same thing. I dared not ask my dad.

It didn't take long for the word to get back to Uncle Ty that I was looking for a package. Maybe a week or so went by and he called the shop while I was there. He must have seen me walking pass his house towards the shop with my friends. We were all hanging outside and Spike came to the door to tell me that I had a phone call. I didn't think too much about who it was. I thought that it was probably Dawana or my mom. When I picked up, it was Uncle Ty telling me to come to his house after all my homeboys left. I didn't hesitate one minute. I told them that I had to do something for Uncle Ty and left them to go straight over there.

He was walking out of his front door when I walked up his driveway. It didn't look like he was in a good mood at all. He walked over to his car and told me to get into the passenger side as I got closer. I thought something had happened or I was in trouble for something. When I sat in there, he handed me an ounce of weed in a sandwich bag and told me to put it in my pocket.

As much as I was determined to get my hands on a package, when it finally touched my hands, fear set in. You know, life is all about choices and once you commit to any particular decision, you have to do just that most times-commit.

"Now Pete you sure this what you want to do?" Uncle Ty said while he glared at me with his stern face. It made me a little nervous. His eyes change colors when his mood changes; really. I knew he would have taken it back if I would have changed my mind right then, but I couldn't push myself to ask Big Mike for another dime. I just didn't want to go through that ever again.

Uncle Ty gave me the game. He made me swear that I wouldn't tell anybody where I was getting it from, especially Big Mike. I forget what to he told me to bring him back, I can't remember what it was, but he was adamant on me bringing him his money when I got it. We sat in that car and spoke for about an hour. Very little of that conversation was about selling drugs, and more about the grown man decision I was making.

"...I rather you get it from me than one of these clowns on the street Pete. They been telling me that you been hunting for something. These streets ain't nothing play with son. You almost grown, you gotta live for you, but I don't want to see nothing happen to you. The first time you do something stupid, Imma cut you off and you won't be able get ya hands on nothing round here..." Unc really didn't want to give it to me. I broke his heart that day, but like he said, he rather me get it from family than from someone who didn't care anything for me out in the street. That was the day I started selling drugs. If I could go back to that moment in the car, I would have told Uncle Ty that I didn't really want to do it. I never knew that decision would cost me and the people I love so much. I was almost fifteen.

Unc pretty much left it up to me to figure it out. When I left his house that day, I went straight to Dog's trailer. When I showed Dog what Uncle Ty gave me, it was like he saw a ghost. He was shocked at first, but then he went right into his mode. See Dog has always had a lot of patience and never minded sitting someone down and teaching them something. He pulled out some small plastic baggies from the cabinet and showed me how to bag it up, told me what each bag cost, and showed me what I should make. Just like Uncle Ty, he gave me this long drawn out sermon; I should have listened. That was my second opportunity to never start. Dog would have given me the money to pay Uncle Ty and I never would have sold a thing.

Most times when we make dumb decisions, God has this way of giving us a way out before we get in too deep. A lot of times we're so dead set on doing whatever it is that we're getting ourselves into that we don't even notice.

Hustling weed was easy. Dog was selling crack and coke out of the trailer and had a lot of traffic coming through. He would have weed to sell every now and then, but really didn't mess with it too tough. I would sit in the trailer and serve all the folks that asked Dog if he had any. I was hustling a little bit at school and a whole lot down at the shop. The biggest issue I had was making sure my dad didn't find out.

There was this guy in the hood named Rob Base. Rob was pretty cool, in his mid-twenties, but had some serious habits. Rob smoked crack, sniffed coke, smoked weed-he did everything. Rob was one of the runners in the hood.

Runners are fiends that serve as 'middle men' between drug dealers and customers. If someone nobody ever saw before or someone nobody trusted came to buy drugs, the runner would ask them what they wanted, take their money to the dealer, get what they wanted, and take it back to them. This way the hustler didn't have to deal with the customer directly, so if it was actually the police, they would not have any proof that the dealer actually sold them anything; it was all on the runner. In return for handling the transaction, the runner would get cocaine.

Rob Base was running for Big Mike, Uncle Ty, Dog, and whoever else was selling drugs in Hallsboro. When he found out I was selling weed, he caught me out at the store and told me he would bring folks to me if they wanted some. He already knew not to let Big Mike know. You would always see Rob Base riding through Hallsboro with different people taking them to buy coke. There were other runners around the way, but Rob was the hardest working one.

I remember times Uncle Ty would come to the park to play ball with us; he would have Rob Base with him. While Unc played a few games of basketball, Rob Base would stand at the end of the road and serve everybody who was coming out there to cop from Unc. Uncle Ty would give Rob Base two or three ounces of dope, and by the time we got finished playing, he would have a few thousand dollars for Unc. He never stole one penny and he hustled better than most of the hustlers that didn't smoke. Uncle Ty and my Dad always called him one of the best runners on the planet.

When he started bringing people to me at Dog's and the shop, I started making a little money. It wasn't enough to write home about, but it was a couple hundred dollars a week. That was more than what Uncle Ty was giving me before, and the biggest thing, I didn't have to ask my dad for nothing.

I did a good job of hiding the fact that I was hustling. My mom didn't have a clue, Big Mike definitely didn't have a clue, and Dawana didn't have any idea. Hustling at school back then was so easy. That was long before they started bringing the drug dogs through schools like they do these days. Before the end of the school day, I usually was making anywhere from fifty to a hundred dollars. May not sound like much money, but for a teenager, that's almost borderline-rich.

Whenever Dawana and I saw each other or spoke on the phone, the world around me would stop for a moment. It was amazing to everybody in my circle for me to be so in love with her, mainly because I was screwing so many different girls at the time. I was a mess, but she was the only woman I loved. I kept her away from Dog's house, and somehow all the girls in school that I was screwing never said anything. It wasn't because I had so much game, I thought so, but somehow it just didn't get back to her. I know, I was a piece of crap.

As for my mom, she was tired. Big Mike was traveling a whole lot more since Julio and Paquito got jammed up. The traffic coming to the barn was literally out of control. People came in droves from sunup-to-sunup. When he was home, he spent most of his time in the barn. Him sleeping with a whole lot of women went from being just rumors, to my mom finding phone numbers in his pockets when she would wash his clothes. A lot of times, women would come to the barn and stay for hours. It wasn't anything unusual, people always were hanging out at the barn, but some of the women he was dealing with didn't really make too much of an attempt to be low key.

Of course my grandmother tried to talk to my mom a million and one times. She even talked to Big Mike over and over. But you know how it is when a woman is fed up. There's absolutely nothing anybody can do about it; nobody but God. My mom packed her and Tracy's things. They left and got an apartment in Whiteville-again. Dealing with the murder of her sister and Big Mike's shenanigans, it was all just too much. She held up for as long as she could, but everybody has a breaking point. Now it was just my dad, Mont, Rooster and I.

You would have thought that Pop would have been really hurt, but nah, that wasn't the type of guy he was. He didn't skip a beat. The traffic coming to the barn was wide open, and to give you an idea on how things were on Red Bug at the time....well, it looked like a lane of I-95 was running straight through Hallsboro. Big

Mike still would go out of town and stay for weeks at a time, and when he was home, he would throw these huge parties. The fact that he had three young men at the house alone didn't matter. He knew we were well taken care of, financially at least.

Me and Rooster were so involved with sports during that time. That's the thing that really kept us occupied. Coach Mobley was more like a father figure to us than anything else. He knew what Big Mike and my Uncles were doing, but didn't really have an idea on what extent. He was more concerned with making sure me and Rooster excelled on the field and in school. He knew that our talent could take us to any school we wanted to go in the next few years.

Dog's trailer was off-the-chain around this time. He was selling a few thousand dollar's worth of cocaine out of there a day, and every single night was like a party. We would drink and smoke weed until the wee hours of the morning. We had girls from all over the county coming through there. Most of them knew us from playing sports, others were coming because they knew Dog was making a ton of money and partied every night. Whatever the case, there was always more alcohol than we could drink, more weed than we could smoke, and more females than we could handle there. We were a wild bunch. We would videotape some of the orgies that happened there. Most of the women we were dealing with were grown (over 18), but some of them were in school with us. I'll never forget, one day the principle called us into his office. Somehow one of those videotapes got out, was floating around school, and got into his hands. We didn't get in trouble, I really don't think there was a specific rule we had broken at the time, but it was embarrassing. I thought for sure we were going to jail when I walked into that office and saw that tape lying on his desk.

We needed a name for ourselves. Everybody already knew that we were a crew, but we wanted to be identified as something. That's just what people did in those days; they always came up with a name. Well Dog had given us this old car to ride around in. It was a 2-door silver Chevy Starlet that was a couple years old. Wasn't really beat up, but at that time you really didn't see people driving them around anymore-it was a hooptie. That was the main source of transportation at the time for the crew, and all the girls we picked up to bring over. It was only natural that we called ourselves 'The Hooptie Crew'.

Getting people to recognize our new moniker was a little difficult. One day after school we all went to the trailer like we usually did. Dog and Joe met us at the door, both grinning from ear-to-ear. When we walked in he had black hoodies for all of us with our names on printed on them and 'The Hooptie Crew' printed on them. We thought we were superstars. Everywhere we went together, especially the ones of us at school, we had on our hoodies. Not long after, the girls who hung out with the crew, the 'Hooptiettes', got hoodies. We were already the most popular kids around, but with the establishment of 'The Hooptie Crew', our popularity escalated to another level. More people started coming to the trailer to hang out, we were doing a lot more drinking and partying; we were the hot boys at the time.

With all that partying, it was inevitable that my school grades would start to decline. That's exactly what happened. I never really applied myself in school, but by basketball season of my tenth grade year, my grades were at an all-time low. My grades were too low to even play on the team that year. For the first time in a long time, I felt like the biggest fool on the planet. Uncle Ty was disappointed; Dog was so disappointed that I think he went a few days without even speaking to me. Dog always encouraged us to keep our school grades straight and to excel in the books, regardless of how much we partied. It wasn't his fault; it wasn't anybody's fault but mine. Being a failure in Dog's and Uncle Ty's eyes was bad, but it felt even worse when Dawana found out. I remember telling her over the phone and listening to her cry. She hadn't found out that I was a straight boy-whore or that I was selling weed, but something like my grades almost caused her to leave me. I managed to keep her for a little while, but the way she felt about me was certainly different. She stopped talking to me so much on the phone after then. What used to be long hours on the phone until it was time for her to go to bed, turned into thirty minute phone conversations a day; always ending with *"Petey I'm bout to go do my homework, you should do the same."*

CHAPTER 8 – THE HOOPTIE CREW

Somehow, I managed to get my grades up that year just in time for baseball season. Me and Rooster were the two best dudes on the team, but I'll be honest, Rooster was something special. He had scouts coming to see him from some of the best schools in the country and we were just sophomores. When they came to see him, it was only natural that they had an opportunity to look at me as well. Uncle Ty would come to all the games and support us. He was proud of how well we'd played. There were a few months that my dad stayed completely gone that year. We didn't see him at all. The only way that we knew he was ok was Uncle Ty telling us that he'd spoken with him. A lot happened during that year, but by the grace of God I was passed on to the 11th grade. The coming summer would be one of the most memorable summers of my entire life....

The 'Hooptie Crew Headquarters', Dog's house, was all the way live from the beginning of the summer. By this time, I had established a few consistent customers and was making a lot more money. Being at Dog's house all day made it easier for people to come cop from me and by this time, the fiends who were buying cocaine and crack from Dog knew I had weed so they would buy from me as well.

Partying turned into a twenty-four-seven deal at the trailer. People from all over were just coming to hang out because Dog didn't really care how old you were, if you came, you could drink and smoke as much as you wanted-if you weren't too young. Most of the people coming were girls, cousins, and some of the other athletic standouts from around the county anyway. If you were cool with one of us in the 'Hooptie Crew', you could come through and chill. Now that I'm older, it amazes me how many women over eighteen I was sleeping with. Some of them were in their midtwenties around that time, and I was just on my way to being a Jr. in high school.

We hung out a lot at the park then. Most of the time we would be playing ball while other times we would just be hanging out. You know how summers can be with girls wearing the shortest shorts and skirts they could find and everybody wanting to be outside. The park was packed all day every day that summer.

I spent a lot of nights at the trailer. I would always go home in the mornings and check on Mont when Pop wasn't there, but most nights, me and Rooster would be in that little trailer partying our asses off. Everybody in the Hooptie crew was planning to go down to Myrtle Beach for the 4th of July that year. The plan was to get a few rooms for a couple of days and have the time of our lives, so I needed to make some money. Dog would have paid for everything, but I wanted to pay for my part with my own money.

As usual, Big Mike wasn't home so after I checked on Mont one morning, I bagged up my entire weed package and got all my money together. The 4th of July wasn't that far away, so I wanted to make as much money as I could; quickly. As soon as it got around the time people would start showing up at the park, I walked down there with my weed and my money. I didn't have any plans on playing basketball; all I was focused on that day was hustling.

One of the first people I saw was Juice. We hardly ever went out to the park that early, so I was kind of surprised to see him out there. From the looks of it, he wasn't too concerned with playing any ball either; he had on a pair of jeans. He was off to himself chilling under one of the trees, so I walked over and kicked it with him.

We chopped it up for a few and I told him what the deal was for the day while I pulled my money out to count it. *"Yo, I need to get up about eight-hundred dollars before the 4th. We goin' be down there the whole week and its goin be broads down there from up and down the whole East Coast. I'm trying to smash every fine one I lay my eyes on..."* I said, while I counted my little cash which was no more than about two-hundred dollars.

Before I got finished counting, a car pulled up to the park and Juice just started walking towards it. ***"P, I'll be right back."*** He said, while he walked towards the passenger side and dug in his pocket for something. When he got into the car, it hit me. I'd seen that car come to the barn and Uncle Ty's shop a few times; it definitely was a dope fiend driving.

Juice sat down in the passenger side for about a minute and the next thing I knew he was hopping right back out the car coming towards me. Well, you don't have to have a degree from Yale to figure out what was going on; Juice was hustling.

When he got back to me, my eyes were big as two bottle caps staring at him; I was almost speechless. Juice just came and started up a conversation about something pointless and started counting some money he pulled out of his back pocket. His little stack was a whole lot bigger than mine.

"Juice!!! How much damn bread is that?!?!" I couldn't help but ask. There were people already at the park congregating and they were already looking our way because he'd just served somebody. He took a step closer to me and turned away from where everyone was looking... ***"Man damn! Why you got to be so dag on loud fo'. I got bout a thousand. This cocaine is a whole nother monster playboy."*** He whispered, but he had some emphasis on the fact that cocaine was another TYPE of monster.

Uncle Ty, Dog and everybody else who mattered that knew I was selling weed, had warned me to stay away from cocaine. I hadn't ever questioned their reasoning. I never once even thought about selling crack, because I'd been seeing what my dad, Uncle Ty, Dog, and everybody else who was hustling was dealing with since I was a small child. But when Juice showed me how much money he had, that was it. I was going to start selling crack, and there was nobody on planet earth that could have told me any different. I didn't even bother asking Juice where he was getting it from, my last name was Powell. It had to be from Pop, Ty, or Dog. More than likely it was Dog. My dad and Uncle Ty would not be too thrilled about giving someone that young cocaine to sell. Just like I thought, it was Dog that was giving it to him. Juice told me after we talked for a few.

That's when I got on my mission. I wasn't worried about selling the little bit of weed I had, I wanted crack-right then. I knew I couldn't go to Uncle Ty, it was breaking his heart that he was letting me sell weed. I damn sure wasn't going to Big Mike. Dog was really my only option. I stayed talking to Juice for a while, but I couldn't wait around too long. I ended up walking straight to the trailer.

Dog was still half sleep when I got there, guess he had a rough night, but I got straight to business. ***"Dog, how you goin' give***

Juice a package and not give me one? Ain't like I won't goin' find out. He down at the park right now-pocket full of money!" After I said that, he rolled his eyes in the back of his head and laid back down on the couch. He was half-way sleep on it watching a college football game when I came to the front door.

"P, you been hustling all this time, I thought you was good. You ain't never said nothing to me about wanting no work. Juice ain't been out there too long. I ain't give him nothing to get rich with. He just was trying to make a few dollars. You jealous or something? What's up man? You ain't ready for that life."

Like always, he was trying to deter me from making another bad decision, and once again, I wasn't trying to hear it. I didn't think Juice was any smarter or more of a hustler than I was, I just wanted on. After a few hours of begging and pleading, Rob Base came to the door. He had somebody outside that wanted some dope from Dog.

He got whatever he came to get from Dog and looked over at me and said, *"Hey Pete, you got some bags on you? I they want a dime of weed."* With his deep country drawl. As I pulled the dime out of my pocket, I had to say it, *"Base, can you tell this man that I'm ready to sell some dope?!?!"* It kind of took Rob by surprise, but he shook his head up and down.

"Dog, Pete doing good with his little weed hustle. He out here making a few dollars, ain't doing nothing stupid. Give the man a little something; I'll keep him straight home boy." He said.

He gave both of us the money for everything he came for and before he left out he told me to get up with him when I had my hands on some work. Dog stood there looking at me for a few moments and then walked back towards his room. When he came out, he was moving with a purpose and had his digital scale and a ziplock bag full of dope in his hands. He sat down at the table and screamed for me to come sit down. Just like it was when I got my first package of weed, I was nervous.

"You wanna be grown, Imma give you a half ounce of hard (crack), and see what you goin' do with it".

He didn't even look up at me when he was trying to weigh it on his digital scale. He was already frustrated that I had begged him for it in the first place. He wasn't mad, but he wasn't in the mood to give me a long drawn out speech about why I shouldn't do it. I sat there and watched him weigh it out; fourteen grams.

"Let me guess P...you don't know how to cut it up, what a dime is, what a twenty is, or nothing huh?" As he shook his head and tied up the ziplock bag he had the rest of the dope in. After he put it back in his room, he sat there and showed me the game. That's the part of him that'll probably never change;

teaching. If you were willing to learn, and he knew he wasn't going to be wasting his breath, he would teach you anything that he knew a little something about.

It had only been about an hour since Rob Base left, and he was knocking on the door again. When Dog opened it, he told Base that he was about to take a nap and he was going to let me handle things for a few. I hopped right into action, and Base didn't skip a beat.

"Boss man gimme a forty. You goin' be right here or you going up the road?" he asked. I quickly replied *"Imma be right here, bring 'em through."*

"Aight Pete, you bout to make some real money now home boy. I'll be back in a little bit." He said as he hurried out the door. Dog had walked back to his room already, so I sat there and watched television awaiting Rob Base's return.

Between Rob Base coming back and all the people that were coming to cop from Dog, I was almost out by the time Dog woke up two hours later. He only wanted six-hundred dollars for the half ounce he'd given me. I had already made the six I owed him, and had made a few hundred dollars for myself. That was the fastest money I'd ever made in my life at that point, but I was the only person that thought it was a big deal. Dog wasn't surprised at all. He was making money that fast every day.

So here I was with the money I'd just made, the weed, the money I already had, and I still had a little crack to sell. There was so much anxiety going through me at the time, I don't even think I could think straight. Dog asked me if I wanted another half-ounce. I'd made so much money so fast, I felt like getting another one was the right thing to do. So that's what I did. There was one catch though...

"Pete, I can't let you sit here and make all my money. It don't work like that home boy. Go up the road. It's plenty of money out there." He said. That's what I did. He gave me another half-ounce and cut it up for me.

When Rob Base came up the next time, I told him that I wanted him to walk up the road with me. He didn't mind at all. I just had to give him a little something-maybe a dime to keep him happy. On the way walking up the road, Rob schooled me to the game, and really stressed how important it was to not let my dad know what I was doing-at all cost. He didn't know what Big Mike would have done to him if he would have found out that he was running for me. To be honest, I don't know what he would have done either.

When we made it to the park, Juice was still standing there. I told him what had just happened and that it was on. Juice felt like we were both about to be filthy rich. I didn't want to intrude on what Juice was already doing at the park, but he explained that there was more traffic coming through there than he and the other guys from my dad and Uncle Ty's crew could handle. We just shared sales. He would serve one car, I would serve the next. Rob Base stood at the road and walked up and down Red Bug - on his job. That was the beginning of what would eventually become all of our downfalls...

We hustled like there was no tomorrow. Big Mike didn't find out. Uncle Ty found out, but he wasn't as mad as I thought he would be. One day he pulled me to the side after he was playing ball at the park and had that conversation with me. He didn't want me to, but I guess his thought was-what could he really say?

Right before we all went down to the beach for the 4th of July, Friday came in town. Friday was Dog's nephew. He lived in Washington D.C at the time, and was one of the most feared men in D.C. He was around six-foot-four, and didn't play. I don't think he played the radio. Rightfully so, people feared him because he was the man that you didn't want to see if you owed someone money. Point blank, Friday was a debt collector; not the nice kind. If someone owed you money, and you were willing to pay a nominal fee, Friday was going to collect every dime-by any means necessary. If that meant him breaking a leg, both your arms, shooting you in the stomach, or doing something bad to your family-you were going to pay. Friday always collected his debt.

What happened was…Uncle Ty had just got jammed up in New Jersey. Big Mike was out in Chicago working on some things with one of his connects, and Unc needed some heavy cocaine quick because usually around the 4th of July he would go down to the beach and sell a few kilos. Think about it…Hustlers from all over the south were always at the beach during the 4th of July. As cheap as him and my dad were getting the work, they always would make a ton of money down there. There was a ton of traffic on the highways during then, so dope was kind of easy to transport without getting jammed.

Uncle Ty went to New Jersey to buy a few kilos and got pulled by the Ft Lee Police department. When he got pulled he hadn't made it to pick up the cocaine, thank God, but he did have eighty-three thousand dollars on him and a handgun. They locked him up for gun and gave him hell about why he had so much money on him. They ended up not charging him for having the gun, but they did him dirty, they didn't give him his money back.

Uncle Ty was out of eighty-three grand, and these guys out of Wilmington he was fronting packages to were slow on paying him back for three kilos he gave them shortly before he went to Jersey; too slow. So, Uncle Ty called Friday down. He was tired of playing with them. He would have done something to him himself, but he wasn't trying to get into anymore situations with the police after getting robbed for all that cash by them.

When Friday came in town, he didn't even give himself time to get settled. He went straight to Uncle Ty's and they rode to Wilmington. Without going into too much detail, we'll just say Unc got his money back with a healthy amount of interest, a little extra to pay Friday, and a half kilo.

By the time the 4th came, I had over two-thousand dollars and had gone shopping for a week's worth of new outfits with the entire Hooptie Crew. We all had a pocket full of money, fresh gear, and enough alcohol and weed to last us a month. Dog wanted to pay for our rooms for the whole week, he had a whole lot more cash than all of us, but we all chipped in. We felt like we were made men.

Big Mike made it back in town, so he took Mont down to the beach with him. Only Heaven knows where they were at down there during that week. We didn't see them at all. Most of us had our own rooms, but there were so many parties going on that we were hardly in there anyway. Myrtle Beach was always packed during that week, but Atlantic beach was where it was at. There were beautiful girls everywhere you looked, and they might as well have been butt-butterball naked with the way they were dressing. They had barely anything on. Every night, every club on Atlantic Beach was packed to capacity, and we were there.

One of my favorite cousins down there was Jeff. He was a little younger than Dog, so when they first met, they hit it off. Jeff was raised on the beach and came off the porch early, which is our way of saying he grew up fast. In the early days when my dad and Uncle Ty would go down there, they would see Jeff hustling around our cousin Cowboy's club all night long. Jeff started selling drugs when he was about eleven years old. He was a millionaire by the time he was seventeen. He capitalized on the crack boom early and never turned back. The little money we had in our pockets didn't mean anything when we got down there and hooked up with Jeff. He paid for everything and let us drive two of his cars; a nearly brand new Mercedes and a convertible BMW. I ain't have license the first, but I was driving like I had 'em. Jeff knew everybody who was anybody on the beach, so when we went into the clubs it was red carpet treatment from the time we pulled up. Most of the clubs didn't have valet parking, but when we showed up with Jeff, we would park right in front and nobody would say a word. He was a movie star everywhere we went.

Being around Jeff that week did something to me. It made me want to grow up faster. I wanted to know what it was like to be treated like a king everywhere I went, what it was like to drive the nicest cars, have more money than I knew what to do with and have the most beautiful women I'd ever seen be willing to do anything to just have a piece of me. Cocaine was like having a genie in a bottle. It could get you anything you wanted. I didn't have to watch a movie to see it, I was witnessing it first-hand.

When we got back to Hallsboro, I knew what I had to do. That's the summer I didn't sleep. We partied hard, but we hustled harder than anything else. It wasn't just us, Uncle Ty and my dad were on a completely new level. Uncle Ty got his auto dealers license and put a small car lot right in front of his house. He started out with a few cars, but when he saw how much money he could make selling rides, he bought more and more. My dad already owned a small club in Bolton, but during this time, he put a little more thought into it and actually started making big money out of there-'The El Derado' was the name of it. It was one of the hottest spots in the area. People were already coming from Acme-Delco, Whiteville, Elizabethtown, Leland, Riegelwood, East Arcadia, Chadbourn, and everywhere else to buy dope from him. Now they could come party with him and the rest of his crew at the club on the weekend; that's what they did. That club pumped for a few years, and then my dad closed it for a while. He was making too much money hustling.

When school started back, I'd already bought more than enough school clothes and shoes, and had over five-thousand dollars put up. I was too involved in sports to really do anything else; that was my true passion. Mike Mobley never let me give up on the idea that sports could take me anywhere I wanted to go in life. During the school year, I refused to sell anything. I wasn't about to go through the embarrassment of flunking off the basketball team again. I guess Pop got too lonely, because that's when he brought Kathy from the beach to live with him in the house. Damn she was beautiful, but every woman Big Mike dealt with was beautiful, so she wasn't special at all to him. I will admit though, she was nice to look at for the time she stayed. At first, I only thought she drank and sniffed a little powder, but eventually I found out the truth. Kathy was nothing more than a beautiful crack head that kept her appearance up. She kept her hour glass figure by working out, and Big Mike kept her in nice clothes. She was a refined lady, but all-in-all she was a crack fiend.

We still hung out at the trailer during the school year, which never changed, but along this time Dog was getting so much money it was crazy. These two fiends in the neighborhood would always be at the trailer; Hootie and Weed Hopper. They were older, but they were both cool as a fan. Dog kept them around all the time to run errands do little odd jobs, but Weed Hopper could cook his ass off. He was a cook when he was in the military and never stopped doing his thing on them pots. Dog would always take Weed Hopper to the grocery store at the beginning of the month. You know how it is, food stamps come out at the first of the month, so it wasn't nothing to give a fiend a gram of cocaine for two-hundred dollars worth of food stamps. We ate like kings every day. There wasn't a dish Weed Hopper couldn't make. The days we wanted to eat out, we would just give Hootie the money to go pick up some take out for us in Whiteville at one of the restaurants there.

Dawana and I took a break. I loved her, but with all the girls I was screwing and the partying I was doing at the trailer, I took her for granted. I tried to make sure I called her every night, but that was impossible most times. One thing I did was make sure I spent time with her at school, but I guess that wasn't enough. That's the thing that me and my father had in common. We were neglecting the women we really loved for other women and other things that really didn't matter. The apple really doesn't fall far from the tree.

During that basketball season that year, I would wake up early on Saturday mornings and go down to Uncle Ty's and work out with him. It didn't matter how early I got down there, Rob Base would already be down there shooting the breeze with Unc. That was because Unc would leave Rob cocaine to sell throughout the night. He never stole, it didn't matter how much dope Unc left with him, and he almost always sold out before Unc would wake up in the mornings. We all left packages with Rob Base through the years. If he didn't already have one, he would gladly work your package. It only made sense; he was always walking up and down Red Bug all night. A lot of people joked about him being the mayor of Hallsboro.

One Saturday I jogged from my father's down to Uncle Ty's like normal, and there was a crowd of people standing on the side of the road a little ways up from Unc's. When I got down there to check out what was going on, Uncle Ty was already down there. To everybody's surprise that morning, there was a dead body lying in a field right off of the road.

Everybody was scared to go down there and see who it was, but from the looks of it, everybody thought it was Hootie. Well, everybody thought it was Hootie until Hootie walked up. Rob Base was the loudest person out there that morning. There were about twenty people standing there in the crowd.

"Hootie they were already making funeral arrangements for you and done called your people and told them you had done passed." Rob said.

We were all waiting on the police to get there, but the suspense was killing everybody. We wanted to know whose body it was. We just needed somebody to walk down there and look. That's a job nobody readily volunteered for, until Rob got tired of waiting and broke out walking towards the body. There was a dead silence in the crowd while he took that walk. You could literally hear Rob's footsteps as he walked over the half frozen leaves that were scattered on the road that ran beside the field. The body was right on the road about 40 yards off of Red Bug.

As he got closer, he slowed down and tried his best to see who it was without having to walk all the way up on the dead body. Then, in all that silence, he screamed out who it was. His words echoed a little through the morning fog when he screamed out, ***"It's Joe Powell!"***

All you heard was gasp and women in the crowd saying, ***"oh God."*** It wouldn't have been so bad to hear that morning, but Dre was standing out there, Joes son. The second he heard Rob Base scream out his father's name, he just turned away and started walking down Red Bug. A few people tried to comfort him, but Dre' wasn't trying to stick around at all. Joe had gotten out there and started using drugs, but him being murdered put a dark cloud over the hood for a little while. The sad part is that Joe and Dre had just began getting warmed up to each other. To make matters worse, the coroner's report revealed that it was death by asphyxiation. Now, there was a murderer amongst us in the little town of Hallsboro. Till this day, nobody knows who killed Joe Powell.

Dog took the death of his brother kind of hard at first, but his nerves of steel didn't allow his emotions to get the best of him. He paid his respects and kept hustling. That seemed to be all of our response to everything; HUSTLE. It seemed like hustling was therapeutic in a sense. It was where we felt comfortable. It was one of the only spaces in our lives that we felt like we had control.

Death makes the wise question their mortality. I'd like to think that's what my father did after Joe died. After he was buried, my dad started going to visit my mom in Whiteville. He would go a few times a week and try to get her back, but she wasn't hearing it. Word got back to her that Kathy was living at the house, and she heard about all of his wild parties. Someone, or a few people, were telling her everything. As much as I knew my dad loved her, he couldn't control the fact that she was just tired.

Me and Tim got a lot closer that year. We hung out more than anybody else in the crew except for me and Dog; especially when I got my license. Tim lived down the road at Lake Waccamaw but he was always at the trailer. Often times when I just wanted to get away from Hallsboro, I would go pick up Tim and we would ride to Whiteville or Wilmington. Sometimes, we would just ride around drinking and smoking. Skirt chasing was a constant activity.

As far as Uncle Ty's love life, he'd gotten married and was having children, but nothing could slow him down. Being the ultimate hustler he's always been, having a family just made him want to make more money. He loved his wife and his children, but he had an ongoing love affair with dead presidents since I was old enough to remember. That year in school, the entire Hooptie Crew excelled. Our grades were a lot better than they'd been the previous year. Mike Mobley and everybody in Hallsboro were proud of what we did on the court and on the field. Scouts were coming to our games from some of the top colleges, and we gave them a show every game. As far as attendance in class, well, that's were money came in. We would skip school all the time, but it cost us. We would go to homeroom in the morning most times, but on the days we skipped to go hook up with some girls at the trailer, mostly grown women at that time, we would pay the school secretary to mark us present in the computer system. We would pay some of the kids in class to do our work for us or get us our assignments. Some of the teachers hated it. They knew exactly how we were not getting docked for attendance, but they never went to the principal. Some might say they were afraid of us because of what my family was doing. In all reality, if we would have gotten in trouble, nothing would have ever happened to them, they were just doing their jobs. On top of that, my dad and all of our parents would have been mad as hell at us.

Me and Dawana got back together later that school year. After basketball season, a lot slowed down for me. I would still hang at the trailer, but I made a conscious effort to make sure I didn't neglect her. I loved the ground she walked on, and when she gave me another chance, I showed her just how much she meant to me. I didn't necessarily stop sleeping with all those girls, but I slowed down quite a bit and focused on her. I would go to meet her at one of her cousin's house when she would spend the weekends over there, when her cousin's parents weren't home. Usually we would just sit and talk or watch television. Dawana loved to kiss, but it never got any more intimate than that; I didn't mind at all. My relationship with her wasn't built on sex or anything like that, that's what made her so special. She was still unaware of my sexual rendezvous with other women. She had no clue what type of life I was living away from school and regardless of what she heard about my family, she never mentioned a thing. She was a constant reminder that I didn't have to live my life the way I was living; an Angel to say the least.

CHAPTER 9 - DECISIONS-JUST ONE TIME COULD KILL

The first day of my 11th grade summer, I was right back at it. The little money I'd saved the summer before was completely gone. I wasn't worried; the only thing I had to do was get Dog to get me on my feet again. Rob Base knew school was out so he was waiting around for me to get my hands of something and start grinding. Dre and Juice were already hustling day to day throughout the year, so they were already into the swing of things.

I'd been telling Dog that I was ready to get on my hustle for a few weeks before school got out. He kept telling me that he had me, but never really slowed down long enough to tell me what the game plan was. When I went to the trailer that day, he gave me an ounce of crack. It was on again.

That summer, we partied less and grinded more. It was like everyone had an epiphany and decided to try to make more money than they ever made. Traffic was coming like crazy and we all were making money hand over fist. Uncle Ty was selling cars faster than half-priced Beyonce concert tickets. He was selling cocaine even faster. My dad was in and out of town bringing cocaine in from eve-rywhere. Then in mid-summer it happened... the drought came.

Finding cocaine was hard. The traffic in Hallsboro kept com-ing, and to be honest, there was more traffic. My dad and Uncle Ty had more than enough cocaine to supply the dealers from sur-rounding areas, but all the other local connects that people would cop from were hurting bad. If they were able to find cocaine during that time, the price was so high that it was ridiculous. The price of coke was through the roof, and the quality wasn't worth a damn. My dad and Uncle Ty were ok because they had connects all over the country that they dealt with. When my dad's connect in D.C didn't have it, he would go to New York. If his connect in New York wasn't able to give him what he wanted, he could go to his connect in Chicago or Alabama.

Dog was working extra hard capitalizing on the drought, but a lot of times he wouldn't be home for me to go re-up from him. Hours would go by before I was able to get more crack. Those few hours meant a lot of money for a small timer like me. Sometimes, Dog would even go out of town for a few days and I was stuck with nothing.

During one of those times Dog went out of town, I ran com-pletely out of dope. Uncle Ty was down at the beach during the time, but coincidently, Big Mike was home. My hustle was going so good, I couldn't even imagine being without dope until Dog or Uncle Ty got back. I didn't have a choice.

I woke up one morning and peeped out of my window to see if my dad was home. His Jag would be parked right on the side of the house in front of my window, it was sitting right there. Kathy was up and moving around, so I thought it was the perfect opportunity to catch him alone. I walked into his room and didn't see him. He was in his bathroom with the door closed.

"Pop! I gotta holla at you about something when you come out aight?" At first he didn't say anything; sometimes he was funny like that.

"Whats up Pete?" His voice sounded somewhat hollowed coming through the door. *"I'll speak to you when you come out."* I replied. I just sat on his bed and waited.

When he came out, I got straight to the point as much as I knew how...*"My home boy wants to get an ounce of hard, but he say ain't nobody got nothing and wanted me to ask you."* I said, and turned my head towards the television because I'd never talked to him about anything like that before. I was pretending to watch whatever was on t.v.

"Yea, is it the same home boy that be working the hell out of Rob Base all day and night? You know, he be over there at his Uncle Dog's and stay the night over here

sometimes and think I don't know what's going on?" He said while he lifted his head to the side and cut his eye at me.

I was caught. *"Yea, but what I'm supposed to do? Be broke while everybody else around here always got money in they pocket. I don't want to ask you for nothing and you know it. You don't want to give me no money without fussing about it."* I said.

"Give me seven hundred dollars. You been hustling and actually thought nobody wont goin' come back and tell me? I know a whole lot more than you think I do. I ain't no dummy. I been round these woods a long time." He said. I was just glad he didn't flip out.

"I got it right here." I reached in my pocket and counted out seven hundred off my little bank roll. It was a weird feeling giving my father money for a package. This was probably the deepest thing that ever happened between me and Big Mike at that point. Bitter-sweet is probably the best words that can describe what was happening. My father, the man responsible for bringing me into the world, was selling me an ounce of crack. He didn't talk to me about the birds and the bees, didn't show me how to play basketball or anything, but here he was selling me drugs. Regardless of how distant or abstract our relationship was, I loved him.

He walked me out to the barn, served me what I came for and before I left out the door, he said *"Son be careful out there.*

Let Rob handle all them faces you don't know." "Ok." I replied and walked out the door.

From that moment forward, I bought my work from Pop and Uncle Ty. Dog didn't have an issue with it at all because he was actually cutting into his profit selling me what I was getting from him. His package wasn't really big enough to be doing that all the My dad liked to have had a heart attack when Unc told him that he was going to get one for me, Big Mike didn't want to buy me a car. He'd bought people cars before but like always, he had an issue with giving me anything. SMH. Ty ended up buying me a mustang. Sometimes he felt more like a father than Big Mike.

The thing that blew my mind that summer is my dad let me hustle out of the barn. That was cool, because when he was gone, I always made a few thousand dollars over those few days. I never had enough crack to serve all the people that were coming so Dog, Juice, and Dre would come over to help me when he was gone. He never left me any of his work to sell. That was a big no-no for Pop.

Dog had traffic coming from all over, but there was this one guy who used to come from South Carolina to cop work from him. He would always have his girlfriend with him. Now, she was fine. We would all try to peep at her if she stayed in the car when her boyfriend came, and if she got out, seems like all of us would get where she was in eyes view. She was just a sexy-gorgeous sight.

One of those times that my father was gone out of town and we were all in the barn, the guy showed up with her. There was always a whole bunch of people coming in and out of the barn, so it was normal to have fifteen or twenty people waiting to get served there. Right before they came, there was another guy from South Carolina that came to get work. We really didn't know him too well, but he'd been there a few times to see my father, so I thought he was cool. The thing about him that day was he just sat there all quiet, hanging around after we served him. Tim noticed that it was strange first and came over to me and brought it to my attention. To be honest, we thought he was plotting to rob us, so I had Tim, Juice, and Dre to go upstairs and get the pistols.

The other guy that was copping from Dog left with his girl-friend. That's when I approached the suspicious dude and asked him what he was waiting around for. When I was speaking to him, everyone else's eyes were on me while they had their hands on their guns tucked up under their shirts or in their pockets. He knew something was real wrong.

"Nah man, I just gotta tell ya'll. That guy who just left is from round my way. He always come around to different spots and bring that girl with him. Yo, he got full blown AIDS and after a while, she'll start coming around by herself. She fine as hell but she sick man.

Imma just warn you, don't mess with that girl if she start coming round."

That blew our minds. We asked him a whole bunch of questions about the guy and his girlfriend but he basically said that the bottom line was-don't mess with her. We'd never seen her come around by herself so we weren't too worried, but we were glad that he told us. If she would have showed up by herself, we probably would have messed with her. She was that fine.

A few weeks later while we were having one of our Hooptie Crew shindigs, Rob Base came knocking at the door. He was happy as hell talking about he was about to hook up with this bad woman. We really didn't pay him too much attention because we had a house full of women and were all drunk. Rob Base just wanted a little something so he could give it to whatever woman he was about to smash. I think Dog may have given him a twenty dollar rock or something, but no one was really paying any attention.

Tim pulled up right after Rob left with whoever he was riding with. We'd sent him to the store on a beer run with Weed Hooper. When Tim and Weed Hopper walked in, Tim busted through the door and loudly said, *"Yo, was that Rob Base leaving?"* We were all staring at him by this time because he was talking so loud. We told him it was Base.

"Damn man, what the hell wrong with Base? He was riding with ole' girl who got AIDS that be coming through with her boyfriend." You could hear a pin drop after he said that.

We'd told Rob what the guy had told us about her. None of us could figure out what the hell he was thinking. It's hard to say, but I believe that's the day Rob Base became a dead man walking. He was a good dude. He ended up dying of AIDS within two years.

I saved up about ten thousand dollars that summer. As for my mom, she was lonely over there in Whiteville. My dad was still going over there a few times a week, and they were slowly but surely working things out. Kathy's days were numbered, and she knew it. She ended up getting my father to take her back down to the beach and shortly after, my mom and Tracy came back home.

That school year, with my mom and Tracy being back, things changed. I can't sit here and tell you that Big Mike became a family man, but he did stay home a lot more. He didn't stay away for weeks at a time and quite honestly, he made his first attempt to stop hustling.

Pop slowed down. People were still coming to the barn, but he rarely let anyone stay too long. After he served them, he would send them on their way. The only time he really stayed out in the barn was when Spike, Uncle Ty or his friend Rambo came over. Like always, they would sit out there and drink and clown around.

We still did our Hooptie Crew thing down at Dog's trailer, but Dog was spending a lot of time out and about trying to expand his business. For the most part, he was in Whiteville doing his thing. Dre and Juice would hustle out of the trailer when he was gone so the traffic was still coming at a rapid pace.

School, sports and Dawana were the main things I focused on. That year Mike Mobley kept us all in check. He knew scouts were looking at us and had a good feeling that a few of us would get scholarships that year. He made us play harder than we'd ever played and put us through the most intense practices known to man.

All eyes were on me and Rooster that year. During basketball season, Rooster almost lost any shot he had. Right after school before a big game, Dog picked me and Rooster up. He wanted to ride to Whiteville real quick to go to J.S Mann's, a men's clothing store in town, to pick up a new outfit to wear to the game. I needed some new sneakers anyway, so me and Rooster hopped in the car. Dog surprised me when we were at the cash register at the store. He paid for my shoes and told me I better play my heart out that game.

On the way back to the trailer, I got Dog to drop me off at home because I had forgotten my clothes and I needed to hop in the shower real quick. After I got myself together I waited on him and Rooster to come, but they were taking all day. Coach Mobley didn't play when it came to being on time before a game. I had to end up getting my mom to drop me off at the school. Rooster didn't make it to the first two quarters, then around half-time I found out. One of my classmates walked by the bench and told me what happened.

When Dog and Rooster dropped me off, they went straight to the trailer. Hootie and Dre were already inside at the time. When Dog and Rooster pulled into the driveway they noticed lights flashing behind them. It was raining badly that day, so I guess it was hard to make out exactly what it was. It was 2 narcotics agents coming to raid the trailer. They'd been waiting and watching for Dog to come back for a few hours.

They were so hell bent over raiding the trailer that they didn't care to slow down when they raced into the driveway. When they slammed on breaks, not thinking about it being real slippery because of the rain, they couldn't stop and rammed right into the side of the trailer. That was Dre and Hootie's queue to bail out. They ran out the front door and darted for the field beside the trailer. One agent drew his gun on Dog and Rooster while they were still in the truck, and the other agent gave chase to Hootie and Dre. Dre almost made it into the woods, but those woods were too thick; he gave up. Hootie on the other hand could have gotten away. Dre had fallen face first in the mud when he was trying to run through that field. When the agent was focused on getting Hootie because he almost made it into the woods, he walked right pass Dre. When he put Hootie in handcuffs and was walking him towards the house, Dre screamed out *"**Here I am**"*, and raised his hand. Yea, that wasn't too bright huh?

They ended up finding about four ounces of crack and about five-thousand dollars in the trailer. They released Rooster but Hootie and Dre ended up getting locked up with Dog. Uncle Ty had to go bail them out. That was the Hooptie Crew's first run-in with the law. Hallsboro was getting hot and one of Dog's old classmates was the main one turning up the heat. He'd just become the head narcotics agent. Him and Dog had bad blood from their early years in school.

After the raid, the authorities rarely even rode through Hallsboro. They finally had concrete evidence of what was going on in there, and it was like they were giving my family a free pass. Years later, we would come to find out that that's when the FED's began building their case; they were waiting.

Right after that happened, Columbus County Sheriff Department tried their hand at bringing us down. This guy named Grover from somewhere close to Tabor City was facing a dope charge in Columbus County. They wired him up and had him to come buy an ounce of coke from Uncle Ty. Unc had sold him cocaine before, so when he came, Unc never suspected a thing. A few months later a secret indictment came down on him. When they picked Unc up

and he looked at the motion of discovery, he saw that Grover was
the one that got him. You never know who's going to be the one to
get you in the street. It's a sad part of the game but it's the reality.
Unc ended up facing ten months state time. That just gave the Feds
more evidence to build their case.

There was this guy from Whiteville, Joe Hood, that would always come to cop from Dog. When word got around that Dog and
Uncle Ty were facing trial for crack charges, Joe Hood kept coming
around telling Dog that he could break into the evidence room at
the sheriff's office. Joe was a character, so we never took him serious. But then he got in Uncle Ty's ear. When people are facing
time in prison, they're very open to suggestions on how to get out of
it. Uncle Ty and Dog weren't going to snitch on anyone, so Joe
Hood's idea started making a lot of sense. If he could break into the
evidence room and steal the evidence, then their cases would have
gotten thrown out of court. Well, a few days after Joe Hood said he
could do it, there was a big news story about the evidence room at
the sheriff's office getting broken in to. Whoever did it stole all the
drugs and guns in there. Well, they almost stole everything. Uncle
Ty always said he had the worst luck in the world. The ounce he
had in the evidence room was the only drugs the thief didn't take.
Not saying that Joe hood did it, and he's dead and gone now so I
can't ask him if he did or not, but Dog did give him two ounces of
cocaine the next time he saw him. Uncle Ty, with the bad luck he

always talked about having, ended up having to serve the ten months. Almost everyone else who had dope or guns in that evidence room that was awaiting trial had their cases thrown out of court.

Dog was making a big name for himself in Whiteville. When it first started getting warm in 92', the place to be on Sundays was the park in over there. There would be hundreds of people out there. It was a big show for the hustlers. Everyone would wash their cars up and put on their best clothes to come out and chill. It was a low-level 'Playa's Ball' for everyone in the county. It was cool though. There was never much trouble at the park other than the occasional fight that happened on the basketball court.

It seemed like Dog knew everybody. Most of the hustlers and a lot of the women that would come out there would always come over and chat with him for a few. Dog wasn't as personable as 'Big Mike', but he was a people person; that runs in our blood.

At any rate, there was this one cat that use to come out there named Funk. He had a few different cars, all of them were pretty new foreign models, and you could tell he was getting to some money just by looking at him. To say the least, he looked like a seasoned dope boy.

He approached Dog one of those Sundays that we were out there, telling him that he wanted to do some business with him. It threw Dog by surprise because we'd never really had any interaction with the guy. Dog was cordial with him. He seemed like he was cool, but then it happened.

After that Sunday, one of Dog's baby mamas bought the guy's name up and told Dog that she'd heard that they were supposed to be doing business together. That upset him because he was so private about what he did, especially what he did in the street. It made him even angrier that one of his baby mamas had that kind of information. One thing that Dog did know was that he and Funk were sexing a few of the same women.

A few Sundays later, Funk popped back up at the park when we were out there. Just like he did a few Sundays before, he got out of his car and made a b-line straight to us. Dog tapped me to get my attention to let me know that he was walking up. I already had my pistol one me, and Dog had already told me what his baby mama had told him. I just leaned back and kept my cool. As soon as he came over, he told Dog that he was still looking to do business with him. He'd heard of my father, but I really don't think he knew that Dog and my father were brothers. If he would have known, maybe he would have never approached Dog; who knows.

This time, Dog checked him as soon as he started talking about doing business with him...

"Man why you keep pressing me bout buying some damn work from you?!?! I got your number. I told you

I'll let you know if we can do something but damn bruh, you starting to really get on my damn nerves..."

Dog didn't scream at him too loudly, but he was dead serious about what he was saying. Funk was a smooth dude. He just smiled, told Dog that he was sorry for the misunderstanding and walked back over to the rest of his crew that were waiting by his car. We really didn't think too much of it then, we should have. In the next couple of months the repercussions of that simple convo would bring a dark cloud over our camp. As graduation time approached, what Coach Mobley had always told us finally came to fruition. Rooster found out that he had been drafted by the Milwaukee Brewers in the eighteenth round of the draft fresh out of high school. That was one of the happiest moments we had in the Hooptie Crew. It made me realize that beautiful things were possible, but it was bitter-sweet. I had offers to go play baseball at some of the smaller schools in the state, but none that really peaked my interest. Coach Mobley encouraged me to go, but through my eyes drugs looked like a better option at the time. Four years in school playing ball could or could not have gotten me to the big leagues. Four years in the cocaine business could have undoubtedly made me a multi-millionaire. Which one would have been more enticing to you? I'd seen how much money I could make selling drugs my entire life. It was a much more tangible idea.

On graduation day as Tim, Kendal, Rooster, and I sat in the gym waiting to walk across that stage, a million and one things ran through my mind. Rooster's life was already figured out. He was officially a major league baseball player. Kendal had always worked and was planning on going to a community college while he picked up a full-time position at the grocery store he was working at. Might not have been a lot of money, but he was going to be making a descent income while he pursued higher learning. That was an honorable thing to do. Well, Tim and I hadn't figured it out yet. Hell, it was hard enough making it out of high school.

That was a very special day for my family. My mom, sister, Dog, my other Uncles, cousins, grandparents, and even my dad were in the crowd waiting for me to walk across that stage. Having my father there struck a sense of pride deep in my spirit. To top it all off, Dawana was there. I think she cried from the time she made it through the front door of the gym; she almost made me teary-eyed when I saw her.

When I walked across that stage, you would have thought one of the Beatles had stepped into the gym. There were so many people screaming and whistling when my name was called. It was a monumental moment in my life. Once we all got our diplomas and said our goodbyes to our teachers and classmates, we got ready for the biggest party Hallsboro had ever seen til this day; my graduation party.

Before Facebook, before everyone had email accounts, the only way to market any kind of event was word of mouth. We didn't put out any info on the radio, there wasn't even any posters put up through the county letting people know that I was having a party. I didn't even know Big Mike was throwing me a party until the week before graduation. Anyhow, there were over three-hundred people at my party that night at my dad's house. There were cars lined up on both sides of Red Bug from my dad's house to a mile away, going in both directions, and trust me, there's not one ounce of exaggeration in that. Everything was free and there was more than enough alcohol, weed, and food for everybody that came.

Dawana was there. Her mom wouldn't let her stay out really late but she was able to stay for a few hours. As soon as she left it was play time. There were girls and women from all over the county and all the surrounding counties there. Not just any women, I'm talking about the baddest women around. They were all there to celebrate my big day with me. We partied all night long. There were so many women trying to get at me that night, I could barely go to the bathroom without one of them throwing themselves at me. One of them was one of my classmates. She was without a doubt, the finest chick on our side of the county and I'd always wanted to get with her, but the opportunity never presented itself. After everybody left the party that next morning when the sun came up, all I wanted to do was go to my room and go to sleep. On my way inside the house, Tim and Juice came out of the barn and told me that the girl was in there crying her eyes out; drunk. When I walked back into the barn to see what was wrong, the only thing she could tell me was that she'd always wanted to be my girl throughout all those years in school. It took me by surprise because I never had any idea. For the sake of keeping this book as clean as possible, you know what happened next....And after we finished, I took her home.

CHAPTER 10 – HER LAST TEAR

The week after I graduated from high school was difficult in a sense. Most of my classmates knew exactly what they wanted to do, and here I was in limbo. I knew I was going to hustle that summer, that was a given, but I honestly wanted to give a better life a shot. That led me to going to see Coach Mobley. The teachers always worked a couple weeks after school was out. My grades wouldn't allow me to get into any of the schools I really wanted to go to but Coach Mobley reminded me that Clinton Jr. College in Rock Hill, South Carolina had been looking at me during basketball season. He made a call to the coach; it was that easy. I was going to be a freshman in college that fall.

Rooster didn't have much of a break after graduation. He hopped on a flight to Arizona for minor league summer ball. The beautiful part was the fact that they gave him a twenty-five thousand dollar signing bonus. He did well during the evaluations that summer and ended up moving up to the next level of the minors. Rooster was living out his dream.

I knew Dawana was going to be extremely proud of the fact that I was going to school, so I wanted to make the moment I told her special. One day when everyone was gone I called to tell her that I needed her to come over, and that it was very important. It didn't take her long at all to show up. There were probably a million things that were going through her mind when she walked in.

I sat her down on the couch, grabbed both her hands, looked her dead in her beautiful eyes and told her the news. I thought she was going to jump up and down ecstatically, but that didn't happen. She immediately burst out in tears and hugged me like she'd never hugged me before. Her tears wet the whole side of my face and neck. She just held me and kept crying. I never doubted that she always wanted the best for me, but this moment felt realer than any other moment we'd experienced. We didn't say a word, just embraced each other while her tears flowed. That day, she gave herself to me. When she left my house, she was no longer a virgin.

Tim was thinking about going to North Carolina A&T, but when he heard the news of me going to Clinton he decided to enroll there. Having my best friend there just made me a whole lot more comfortable about going. We were set to leave for school in August but that summer, our plan was to stack as much money as we could. It was time to do what we did best.

My dad was still a little shaken about what happened to Uncle Ty. He and my mom weren't on the best of terms and the house wasn't what you would call a happy home. He wasn't the same. Pop almost completely stopped hustling. Traffic was coming to the barn, but he was always turning people away telling them that he didn't have anything. It was a little strange to be honest and then things got even stranger.

I would walk into the barn or the house and he would be sitting around nodding, not really saying much. He would drink and sniff a little, but this was different. I knew something was wrong but I couldn't put my finger on it. See, when Big Mike was turning all of those people away that were coming to the barn, he had coke. He just really didn't feel like dealing with anybody at the time. He knew that he was missing out on major money, but at the time, he could care less.

I knew what I had to do to get my money right to go to school, so of course I went to him. I had just gotten about two-thousand dollars that people had given me as graduation gifts. I knew Tim was going to be with me day-to-day that summer so I bought two ounces of coke from my dad. He didn't have a problem selling it to me, but he shut down for anybody else that came. He spent a lot of time in the barn just watching TV. Sometimes when I would go in there to talk with him about something, he would be nodding off in the middle of a sentence.

I wasn't the only person that noticed the drastic change in him, everybody noticed. No one ever came out and bluntly addressed it, but they knew something wasn't right. My grandmother would come over and check on him. From time to time she would ask me what was going on with him but the honest truth was, I didn't know. The other truth was the fact that I wasn't really concerned because I was too focused on hustling up money to take to school when it began. Things were good in the street for me, especially being able to hustle out of the barn because Pop was taking a hiatus. The only thing that was different from the previous summer was the fact that Rob Base was dead and gone. AIDs took him away from here quicker than everyone expected. Me and Tim were hustling around the clock.

Dog had a bad taste in his mouth about the trailer after the narcotics agents raided, so he bought a small home a little further down Red Bug. It was right at a mile from my father's house and it sat way off the main road. You had to take a long road, almost a quarter mile long, from off of Red Bug to get to the house. There were only two more houses on that road. If you weren't one of the people that lived in those two houses, or if Dog didn't know you were coming to see him, you had no business down there. Dog was tired of all the traffic and this gave him the seclusion he was looking for.

He still kept the trailer for a while. We still did our Hooptie Crew partying there. Juice still hustled out of there and Dog would come for a few hours a day to hustle. He never kept a lot of cocaine up there anymore and he made Juice stash the coke that he was fronting him in the woods behind it. That raid and Uncle Ty getting jammed up made us a lot more cautious.

Me and Tim spent most of our time at the barn. We tried hard to salvage the customers that were coming through there, but it's like Big Mike had a spell over them. If they couldn't deal with Pop, they went up the road to one of his crew or Dog. The dope game is funny like that. A lot of folks think fiends will buy drugs from just anybody; that's not the case all the time. Big Mike's customers were loyal to him. Me and Tim were new faces. They knew I was Big Mike's son but that didn't really matter. On top of that, politicians, school teachers, prominent figures in the area, and people of that nature were coming to get dope from my dad. They didn't want just anybody knowing their business. Regardless of dealing with all of that, Tim and I still made money.

My dad was somewhat reclusive during that time, and though we weren't that close, it was breaking my spirit to watch what he was going through. It was breaking me even more not knowing what was going on with him. There was a dark cloud over our home that was keeping my mother from smiling. The sorrow inside of her was too much to stay there; she had to cry it out continuously. My mom was a strong woman but issues of the heart will break anybody down, no matter how strong they are.

We played the beach heavy that summer. Like always, my family down there showed us love, especially Jeff. Cowboy, Manager, and the rest of my family down there always asked about Pop. He would still go down there from time-to-time, but he wouldn't hang out like he used to. I would always tell them that he was doing ok, but they knew he wasn't.

On one of those weekends the whole Hooptie crew went down to the beach and I saw something that literally blew my mind. We were in Cadillac's one night shooting the bo bo with Jeff and Manager, and Kathy walked in. I was the first one to see her come in,

but it really didn't hit me that it was her until she got closer to me at the bar. She was a hot mess. The once beautiful lady that lived at my house looked like she was at the lowest point of life. She was dirty, reeked of cheap liquor, her clothes were almost falling off of her because of the weight she'd loss; she was skin and bones. To make matters worse, Cadillac immediately frowned up when he saw her and said ***"Kathy don't come up in here begging tonight, and don't be in here being worrisome as hell either."***

It caught me by surprise that he was talking to her like that. I mean, this woman was once my dad's arm piece. She didn't pay him any attention; she was too busy trying to get to me when she noticed me sitting at the bar. As she got closer her arms extended to give me a hug, and I hugged her. Drugs had taken her completely over. My whole crew was speechless. They couldn't believe that she'd let the life get sucked out of her.

She asked about Big Mike and I could tell she was a little uncomfortable speaking to me. She was once full of confidence, now she was trying to hold back all of her insecurities just to have a simple conversation with me. It was a struggle. She left after a few minutes, and all I could think about was my dad. Whatever was bothering him, I hope it wasn't going to drag him down to that point.

When I got back home, I started paying a lot more attention to Pop. We weren't close enough for me to just come out and ask him, but after a few days of really observing him I figured out what was going on with him.

It wasn't nothing to see big Mike sniff coke or get drunk. But after watching him snort a few times over a few days, I noticed that he was nodding out afterwards; every time. Coke doesn't have that kind of effect. Usually after he hit coke, he was hyper. I never went through his stuff; I've just never been the type to snoop through people's things. This time I had to. I knew where he kept his personal coke stash in his room, and I just took a peep. What I saw, well, I'd already had a little notion; was heroin-powder form. That explained the reclusiveness, the nodding out, and why he just wasn't himself. This was the first time life introduced me to heartbreak.

Till this day, I don't know if my mom knew during that time. Quite honestly I don't think too many people knew what was really happening. For me, it made me grow up even faster than I was growing up already. Somehow my mom's tears, my grandmother's motherly concerns, and my father deteriorating in front of my eyes gave me strength. It motivated me to want more out of my own life. School was right around the corner and it was my chance to become more than a drug dealer. Big Mike, as much as I loved him, was a heroin addict. At this stage in my life I couldn't let anything deter me from pursuing something better. Clinton was giving me a chance to play basketball and get an education. My life in Hallsboro, well, I was nothing more than a drug dealer there. My father was dealing with a demon that he had to fight by himself. I had to stay focused on leaving.

Just before Tim and I left for school, we'd finally established a nice flow of customers at the barn. We'd hustle up the street at the shop and at the trailer with Juice from time-to-time, but for the most part we were at the barn doing our thing. Dawana would come over every few days, which was cool but she would have to sneak over during the day when her mom went to work. During that part of the day, there wasn't a lot of traffic. She still didn't have a clue that I was hustling. She wasn't dumb by a long shot, one of the smartest people in her class; she just didn't have any clue about anything concerning that kind of lifestyle. She was sheltered and that worked out perfectly for me.

My parents spoiled Mont like he was their only child. I'll admit it, I spoiled him to. Just like me, he was way more privileged than all of his peers; the freshest clothes, a few dollars in his pocket-the latest and greatest of everything. I bought him a go cart, four-wheeler and a dirt bike throughout those years. He was just a bright kid and we all knew my aunt would have been proud of him. Pop spent a lot of time with Mont during this time. Since he wasn't hustling like he used to, he had a lot of time on his hands. Around then, he bought a small home close to the beach. Heaven knows what he was doing down there but if I had to guess- he was getting high, sexing different women and selling a little coke down there. That was his refuge away from the monotonous day-to-day in Hallsboro.

Dog was still on his grind around the way. He started letting a few people come to his new spot to cop, but only the fiends that he knew really well. Between the new spot and Juice hustling down at the trailer, he was making a killing. His old classmate, the head narcotics agent, had a hard-on for him and was determined to get him. Dog hated him. That was his arch nemesis.

One day Dog and I were chilling in his new crib and out of no-where, there was a loud bang at the front door and five narcotic agents rushing in-guns raised. Just-so-happen, the only dope Dog had was down at the other trailer with Juice. They had the two of us on the floor handcuffed while they searched and searched. Those fools looked for over an hour and couldn't come up with nothing. Just when we started talking crap to them about how they were looking for no reason and violating our rights, knowing we just got lucky, Dog's arch nemesis walked from one of the back rooms with a sixteenth of an ounce of crack.

Dog still says that they planted it on us, but that led them to go outside and check our cars. That was the killer. I knew for a fact that my gun was lying right in the passenger seat under a t-shirt, a small chrome .380. I always kept a t-shirt or towel in there to put over my guns. I never went anywhere without a gun at that point.

They found the gun quickly. All me and Dog could do was sit there and watch in agony. They had both of us now-Dog with pos-session of crack and maintaining a dwelling for the sale of cocaine, and me with a weapons charge. Big Mike bonded us out a few hours after we were booked and of course, he cursed me out with every breath that came out of his body on the ride home.

"Now what you goin do? I want my damn money soon as we get to the M'F'ing house. You better go and find you a good lawyer today and you know I ain't

spending a dime to help yo' black ass out..." He went on and on. I didn't say a word. I was too busy thinking about what had just happened.

The attorney I used cost me fifteen hundred dollars, but it was well worth it. At my first appearance in court, he got the charge thrown out on the account that I was only seventeen and he had a relationship with the judge. The gun wasn't stolen or anything. It was registered to one of the fiends I was serving. We told the judge that he was riding in my car and forgot that he left it in there. I think the judge knew that my story was BS, but he let me go. I felt like I'd just beat a murder case. Dog on the other hand, he was put on intense probation. We got off lucky.

My dad would sell me a few ounces but he never wanted to front me or Dog anything. He claimed we weren't turning money fast enough for his taste. He was fronting guys work from Georgetown, S.C, Latta, S.C, Lumberton, N.C, the beach, Wilmington, Greenville, N.C, Charlotte, and Raleigh; but wouldn't give his own brother or son anything to flip. The bad part about it was, the people he was fronting dope to were slow with paying him. Some of them, just disappeared and didn't pay him at all. He was losing big money, but was so high on heroin all the time; it really didn't seem to bother him. We were watching his ship go down fast, and couldn't do a thing about it.

Tim and I hustled our asses off even more than we did in the beginning of the summer after I beat my case. It was time to go school and we weren't about to be away from home broke. The closer it got to our departure date, the harder we went. Altogether, we had close to fifteen thousand dollars. We would split everything down the middle. When he ate, I ate. When he or I hooked up with a new chic, the other one would have one of her friends. We did everything together. He was my brother, my friend and my business partner. What was mine was his, and vice versa.

The week we left for school, my grandparents gave me a few hundred dollars. They just wanted to make sure I was ok when I was away. I tried not to take it, but they insisted. They didn't know I was hustling. A few of my dad's friends gave me a few dollars, and of course Dog hit me off with a few dollars. He was proud of me and really understood how school was going to keep me out the street and give me a real chance at a different life.

Dog and I rode down to the beach to check on my Pop that week. He'd gone down to his place down there for a few days and it was only right to check him out before I left. The two of us had an interesting conversation on the way there. He'd asked me if Big Mike had given me any money to take with me to school. Dog already knew the answer.

"Pete, Mike goin' give you some money today. He ain't never gave you nothing, shit, he ain't never been in

your life. Bruh, you been with me since you was ten, for the most part. He ain't never did a damn thing for you. I love my brother to death, but if he don't give you at least a thousand dollars today, we going be some fighting asses..." He said.

Dog was dead serious about what he was saying, and he was right. There was a lot of underlying tension there as well. Big Mike could have fronted us a kilo or two and it wouldn't have been a big deal. Instead, he was letting the fools he was dealing with play him. It felt like he just didn't want us to make any real money. On top of that, it wasn't like he was giving us a deal on the dope he was selling us. He was charging us the same price he was charging everybody else. It was good that he would even sell us anything, because he wasn't really hustling hard right then, but damn; he was treating us like everybody else. That would have made anybody feel some type of way. When we got there, he was just like we'd thought he would be; high as hell and nodding out on that heroin. Dog didn't waste any time at all with small talk, he got straight to the point and asked my dad to give me some money for school. What he responded with blew both of our minds, and hurt the hell out of me.

"...I ain't giving him no money. He ain't goin' do nothing but mess it up. I don't know why he even wasting his time going to college for no way. He ain't focused.

He don't care bout nothing. He just goin' 'F' up ..." he said while he looked back and forth from me to Dog.

I couldn't hold back. *"Dog I told you he won't goin' do nothing. I don't know why we came here for in the first place."* I said.

Dog stood there in amazement, but more so than anything he was disappointed. I guess Pop could see the disappointment we both felt.

He stared at us for a quick second, and suddenly walked in his room. He came back with one-thousand dollars. By that point I didn't even want the money, but I took it. Dog told him that he could have given me more. That wasn't a whole lot of money to Big Mike.

We didn't stick around long after that. We said our goodbyes and went back to Hallsboro. I was hurt but I wasn't surprised. I didn't have time to let those hurtful words bother me too much anyway. I had to get ready to leave for school.

I never cried myself a river, because as messed up as this crazy world is; there's always a better day that'll make up for all the screwed up ones. My dad just showed me what he really felt about me, so what. It hurt, but it made me realize that nobody in this world is required to love me-it's a choice. I guess my dad or the heroin in his system, made the choice to not give a damn about me in that moment.

Tim and I still had a little over an ounce of crack left a day before we were headed to Clinton College. We had too much packing and preparing to do to even think about hustling that day, but we couldn't just leave it behind. We'd talked about fronting someone the dope we had left before we left, we just couldn't come to a consensus on who that person was going to be. It ain't like I trusted too many people, and Dog and Juice were working their own package so we couldn't give it to them.

There was this one kid, Dee, up Red Bug that would hustle from time to time. Dee was a junior in high school but he started hustling early; nothing major. He wasn't selling no more than a quarter ounce a week, but that was great compared to all the other hustlers his age. It only made sense to give him a front, so that's what happened. Tim wasn't too happy about it at first because Dee was a little reckless, but we didn't have a whole lot of options.

The college life was amazing. There were a whole lot more chicks at school than we expected, and of course, we started making our rounds through them early. We partied just like we did back at Dog's old trailer, but we weren't fools. We went to class and actually applied ourselves. It felt good knowing that we were actually doing something constructive with our lives for a change.

That little town called Hallsboro wouldn't take it's hands off of us though. We went home every single weekend. Dee was making us a little money, so we had to make sure we picked up more dope for him to sell. Worked out smooth, because he was usually about to run out when the weekend came.

It was good coming home to check in with my family and see my baby, Dawana. Mama was stressed the hell out about my dad, my grandparents were cool, and Dog was expanding his business all over the county. Dawana missed me like crazy through the week and would always spend every free second she had with me on the weekends. Before I left on Sundays she always got extremely emotional. You would have thought I was getting shipped away to Afghanistan the way she cried each time I left.

After my dad told me and Dog what he did at the beach when I went to get the money from him, I really didn't have much to say to him. The only conversations we really had were about cocaine when I went to cop work from him to give to Dee. A couple of times he asked me how school was going and told me to keep up the good work, but that was really it. As smart as my father was, he hadn't really figured out that he was a heroin addict yet. Addicts never understand that they're addicts right away. They always think they have it under control.

When the basketball team started practicing at Clinton, I was able to get the coach to let Tim try out. He was a solid player that I'd played school ball with my entire life and the coach knew he could contribute. That gave me even more reason to enjoy the college thing; my best friend was going to be on the team with me.

I'll never forget the day my mom had enough-for the last time. I called home one night to check in with her and I could tell something was really bothering her from the first few moments she was on the phone. She wasn't really talking much and being short with me. When I asked her what was bothering her, she simply told me that she was finished with my dad.

I sat quietly on the phone and let her vent. We'd never had a real conversation about their personal business. I guess she needed me to hear her out. She'd endured all of those years of my dad's mess, and I totally understood. She still didn't know about his heroin addiction. She was just tired of all the things he'd put her through. The last time she came back, he promised her that he would change. Pop didn't make good on his promise.

My dad was just at a low point. We knew that some of the guys he'd been fronting cocaine to would get missing and not pay him every so often, but no one realized just how long it had been going on. No one realized how long he'd been doing heroin. A lot happened right under our noses; we had no clue. Everybody stayed out of Big Mike's business, so there was no one telling him that he was crashing. The heroin had become his business advisor and best friend. My dad was damn near broke and the woman who loved him more than any other female on this planet was leaving him. This time she was leaving for good.

I tried talking her into staying, but enough was enough. She'd tried being by his side for over twenty years. Everybody has a breaking point. She'd reached hers a long time ago. That next day after class, I drove home to check on my family...

CHAPTER 11 – THE KEY THAT UNLOCKED EVERYTHING

Tim didn't take the ride with me; he figured there was too much on my mind. I sped the whole way there. Seems like the faster I drove the longer it took me to get home. Here I was going to college, and my family was back home falling apart. Uncle Ty was in prison, my father was a heroin addict, my mom was leaving him...

When I got there, no one was home. It really didn't click until I walked inside. As soon as I walked into the house, I felt it-my mom and Tracy were gone. They didn't take much furniture just their personal belongings. My dad wasn't home, as usual. I sat down on the couch in the living room in the dark. My mom plainly told me that she was leaving. I just didn't have an idea that she was going to be moving that fast.

She and Tracy decided to rent a house in Whiteville. Big Mike was at his house down at the beach, so it was the perfect time for my mom to leave without having to go through another argument with my father. They'd moved all of their things that morning, but

I don't know, they may have already been packing when I spoke to my mom the night before.

I ended up going up the street to Uncle Ty's shop. Spike and a few other people were there and all of them were surprised to see me home during the week. Spike told me that he'd seen my mom and sister when they were taking their things out of the house. He knew what was going on but no one else did. Dealing with them leaving was tough enough, but then Spike dropped another bombshell on me.

"Now Pete, that young boy you got hustling out here done got out there bad on that stuff. He smoking heavy cousin." Spike said. That shocked the hell out of me. Dee couldn't have been any older than sixteen or seventeen at the time. It was always sad to see people that young smoking crack, but it become a more common occurrence as time went by. The thing that worried me the most was the fact that Tim and I had just given Dee two ounces of crack two weekends prior. I hopped in my car and set out looking for him. He wasn't at his house; he wasn't at the park or anywhere up Red bug. Dee wasn't anywhere to be found. That wasn't normal. He was always out trying to make a few dollars. That's when it really sunk in that he was smoking.

I was going through a plethora of emotions, but the one that took over was anger. I could have killed him. He never came short on me and Tim's money, but Dog told me before that every now-

and-then he would take our money and buy other packages before we came home on weekend. If he messed our money up, the money he made on the packages he bought would make up for it. Didn't really matter to us, he was bringing us our money. The way Spike was talking about Dee, he was turning into a full-fledged crack fiend.

I had to get the hell out of Hallsboro. I didn't go see Dawana, check out Dog, Juice, my grandparents, or even check out my mom and sister before I left. I hit the road and headed back to school. On the way back, all I could think about was my dad and the house. Big Mike was never home, Mont was nowhere to be found, and there was traffic still coming to the barn. With all those people coming up there, it was only a matter of time before one of them came up with the notion of breaking into the house, especially with nobody there. Also, Big Mike was in need of a serious intervention. His addiction had taken him over and he was at the lowest point he'd ever been in his life. No one really knew what was going on with him, but I knew, and more importantly, I knew that Big Mike needed serious help fast. I needed to leave school and come home.

Telling Tim that I wanted to leave school wasn't an easy thing to do. I told him about what was going on with my mom, Dee, and finally what was going on with my dad. Tim has always had this mature demeanor about him, so he really understood. Just because he understood didn't mean that he was supportive with the idea of me leaving.

"OK-so Dee smoking. He ain't the only person we can get to move dope round there Pete. With your mom, I understand, and I know your dad need you right now. But man, if you quit...that just ain't the right thing to do right now. Might not make much sense right now because I know you feel like you got to do something, but leaving school ain't it Pete." Tim said.

We came to school together, were roommates and on the basketball team, so Tim would be left alone if I decided to leave. My mind was already made up. Our little operation with Dee was about to go south because of his new habit, and the money we had wasn't going to last forever. The decision wasn't really hard for me. When that weekend came I packed my things. I was going back and forth from the car to the dorm taking my things, and Tim just lay in his bed. He asked me if I was sure that leaving was the best thing. I didn't have any other response to give him.

Before I left, I gave Tim about four-thousand dollars. That was fifty percent of the money we had left. I told him that I would catch him around the way when he came home to visit and I walked out. When I hopped in my car and put it in reverse, I looked up and saw Tim running towards me waving me down. I rolled down my window and Tim said, *"Man come on back up and help me get*

my stuff so we can get the hell up outta here." It took us about 30 minutes, then we left Clinton Jr. College for good.

As quick as I became a college student, I became a college drop out. What my father said came to fruition-I F'd up. To make matters worse, Tim came with me. He was ride-or-die, but the reality behind it was that he could have stayed at Clinton, gotten a degree and went on to become whatever he wanted to be. Neither one of us knew what was about to happen. Neither one of us knew that we were headed on a one way street to the federal penitentiary.

The plan was to go home and hustle to keep my father from going all the way down to nothing, enroll at the Southeastern Community College and transfer to a university when I graduated from there. Dropping out of school wasn't supposed to be a permanent thing, I just had more important things to take care of at that time. It was October, so Tim and I planned to enroll at the community college in January.

Everyone was surprised to see us back in the hood. A few of the older folks were a little disappointed, but the fiends greeted us with open arms; they didn't care about what we were doing with our lives-they couldn't think pass getting a hit.

We finally caught up with Dee. He was a mess. He'd already messed up the money. He owed us three grand, only had seventeen hundred, and had smoked up the rest of the package. We wanted to do something bad to him, but it wasn't worth it. It would have been like pissing on ants and we had bigger fish to fry. It was time to get money.

Pop didn't really say too much when I came home. He didn't even acknowledge the fact that my mom had left. He bought a few women who smoked over to clean the house the morning after I got there. They were outside cleaning up, wiping down the walls on the inside, and just cleaning like it was no tomorrow. I was completely thrown off because we never kept a dirty house; it looked like it was spotless already. When I asked him what was going on, he said that the bank was sending an appraiser over because he needed an appraisal for refinancing the house.

The house was already paid for. I couldn't figure out why this fool would even consider getting a loan on it. He was doing a lot worse financially than I thought. It wasn't like he was all the way broke, but when you go from having over a mill to being able to see the end as quick as he did, that'll make anybody panic. Refinancing the house was nothing more than a panic move.

I got three ounces of crack from him. He knew I was about to start grinding hard, that wasn't even anything we had to discuss. When the word got out to the fiends that me and Tim were back in the hood getting it in, they started coming. Tim wasn't really the same when we left school. Hustling didn't excite him like it used to. After a few weeks he felt like it was best that he got a job until he figured out what he was going to do with his life. I really respected how maturely he always thought and it just made more sense at the time. As for me, I was willing to get all the way out there again. He needed time to think about what he was going to do with his life. He ended up getting a job at a plant in Whiteville called Whiteville Plywood. He actually got another one of our homeboys named Chic a job there also. Chic would always be around. His dream was to become a big time rapper, but dreams don't pay the light bill until they happen. He needed some money in his pocket and he didn't want to hustle-smart man.

Dog was still doing his thing in Hallsboro and he was getting money from all the surrounding areas. He spent a lot of time in Whiteville around then. There was this night spot called Ulla Mays that Dog would play on the weekend's real heavy. All the hustlers would congregate there and he would be out there hustling his ass off. A lot of the hustlers who came there would cop their packages from him, and to make things sweeter, he had a little crew in Whiteville that was hustling for him. Dog was like that at the time.

I grinded like it was no tomorrow. When Tim would get off of work, he would come through and chill for a little. We would get on that alcohol and hustle till the early hours of the morning. Most of the time, he would fall asleep at the barn and go straight to work from there.

Dawana was disappointed that I'd just left school. She was empathetic to the fact that my mom left my dad and that my dad had financial problems, but she felt like going to school was more important than anything. Now that I think about it, she never really knew what my father did for a living. She knew my mom would work a lot, but she never really asked too many questions about my dad. She wasn't nosey at all and just wasn't the type to get into anyone's personal business. She was just in the eleventh grade at the time. Her mom was strict, so we really only saw each other on the weekends for a few hours. She heard about what we were doing, but when she came around she didn't pry into our business. When she came around, anything concerning drugs shut down with me. I told her I was just taking time off and was enrolling in school in January. I just needed the time to get myself together. She ultimately understood.

Rooster had a break from baseball and flew into town for what was supposed to be a couple of months. Everyone was happy to see him. Rooster was looking better than he ever did. He was in the best shape of his life, and he had a whole new image with the twenty-five thousand dollar advance they'd given him. Rooster made us all proud.

Around that time Dog and Funk, the dope boy that kept pressing Dog at the park about doing business with him, were at odds and sending messages back and forth by girls they were both deal-

ing with. Here's the thing...there's always going to be certain girls
from an area that like dealing with drug dealers. So, most drug
dealers in certain areas end up messing with the same chics; that's
just how it is. Dog and Funk were dealing with a lot of the same
women.

Dog had a few kids by now, and Funk was dealing with one of
his baby mama's friends. Funk would always tell her how much he
didn't like Dog. Another girl they were both dealing with would always ask Dog why Funk didn't like him. Dog wasn't the type to talk
too much, so he just figured he would handle the situation the next
time he saw him, but the girls would go back and tell Funk little
trivial stuff. Things got real intense, and everybody knew something was going to happen eventually.

One night Dog, Juice, and I went to the projects in Whiteville to
pick up one of Dog's baby mamas. She was going to come to
Hallsboro to spend some time with him, and since we were already
in Whiteville it just made sense to go ahead and pick her up.

When we were waiting outside for her to come, it happened.
Funk pulled into the projects with two other guys in his car. We
couldn't tell exactly who it was because it was dark, but we knew it
was his car. The girl Funk was dealing with was inside the apartment with Dog's baby mama. I guess he was coming over to see
her. They didn't pull up in front of the house because that's where

we were parked, but they pulled into a parking space in front of another set of buildings across from us. They were just sitting there, and Dog and I were looking out Dog's rearview mirrors watching them closely.

A guy named Shane came out of one of the apartments beside Dog's baby mama's and stopped to speak to us when he noticed us waiting there. On his way over to Dog's car he looked across the parking lot. The expression that came over his face was like he'd seen a ghost. He'd noticed that Funk and his boys were parked there. That's when Dog whispered to Juice to give him his gun. Juice was in the back seat, and I don't know why, but it seemed like he really didn't want to give Dog the gun-he was taking forever. Dog wasn't playing at all, he turned around towards Juice and screamed "Give me the damn gun with yo stupid ass!!!" Around that time, all of a sudden, there was a loud noise that sounded like a gun shot. We ducked down and Shane took off running. Funk and his crew were pulling off screeching tires. What happened was, they'd thrown a beer bottle out of their car window and when it hit the pavement it made the noise.

Everything happened very fast, but while we were ducking down in the seat Dog was still screaming at Juice to give him the gun. All I heard then was the backdoor of Dog's car fling open, Juice hopping out, and multiple gun shots ring out right afterwards. Juice had hopped out and was blasting at Funk's car. The scary part was the fact that there were apartments right behind the car as it sped off. I just knew Juice had either killed someone in that car or someone in one of those apartments that were across the parking lot. We just knew somebody was dead. Juice shot over ten times. We sped outta that parking lot and back to Hallsboro like we were leaving the scene of a bank robbery. Dog's baby mama called him later that night and told him that nobody got shot and nobody told the police anything. Thank God. Now, we had a real serious issue. We were going to war with Funk.

Rooster was on a break, but he didn't miss a day of training. He would come into the barn early in the mornings and hit the weights super-heavy. I worked out with him with him a few mornings. It was the most intense workouts that I'd ever experienced. In the evening's right before dark, he would run four or five miles up and down Red Bug.

One of those days about two weeks after he came home, he went on his run as usual. Dog, Juice, and I was taking some dope to one of dudes Dog had hustling for him over in Whiteville. When Rooster went on that run, Funk and two guys were riding down Red Bug looking for us. Like I said, we were at war. They knew Rooster was a professional baseball player, but more importantly to them, they knew Rooster was a part of our circle. What happened next changed Rooster's life forever...

Rooster was on the last stretch of his run and almost back at the house. They pulled up beside him with masks on and held him at gunpoint with a shotgun. They made him lay down in the ditch on the side of the road; put the shotgun to the back of one of his legs, and pulled the trigger. In that instant, Rooster's dream was shattered.

When Dog, Juice, and I came from Whiteville and were driving through Hallsboro, there was an ambulance screaming by us and a crowd of people walking from Red Bug a little ways up from my dad's house. We knew something happened, but we figured it was a car accident or something like that. Right when we came to the stop sign by the park, my homeboy Steim waved us down and came running towards the car. When he told us what happened, the ambulance had already taken off with Rooster. We peeled off headed for the hospital. No one knew how critical Rooster's condition was. A few people in the crowd that was walking actually were screaming and crying because they thought he was dead.

When we got to the hospital we found out that he would be ok, but he had to undergo really serious emergency surgery as soon as he got there. He lost a ton of blood-it was just real bad. In the weeks to come, his leg kept getting infected. It was almost to the point that doctors even considered amputating it.

That night, we loaded up the guns, picked up Tim, and hunted for Funk and anybody who associated with him all night long. We couldn't find anyone. We hunted day and night for the next few weeks and there wasn't a trace of any of them in any of the surrounding areas. He hadn't contacted any of the girls he was screwing that we knew either. We went to every one of their houses. He'd literally disappeared. We even got Friday and some of his goons from D.C to come down to help us look for them. It was an all-out manhunt. We couldn't find them to save our lives.

When Rooster was able to get out about a month later, we were still on a viscous manhunt. Dog got the call one day. Someone knew exactly where Funk was at right then. It was one of them trifling chics that Funk was screwing. On that day, she was smiling in his face, and trying to get him murdered at the same time. She was only screwing him because he had money. She didn't care anything about him. Me, Dog, and Rooster got the guns and were headed straight to him. None of us said too much on the way there. We didn't even have the radio playing. About half-way to Elizabethtown, where he was at, Rooster told us to turn around.

"It ain't worth it y'all. He ain't worth none of us going to jail over, he ain't worth the time. Imma let God handle it..." Me and Dog went off on him.

"Motherfu*$#% we done did all this looking and you talking bout let God handle it!!!" Dog screamed. We just let it go. We turned around, dropped Rooster off at the house, and went

over Dog's crib. We were mad as hell, but looking at it now, Rooster saved us from a murder charge. We would run into Funk a few times over the years, but nothing ever happened. He's always denied that it was him, but now, it doesn't even matter. Just like Karma gave us a visit years later for what we'd done; Karma also made a stop to see him...

By this time, I was making a killing at the barn. My dad wasn't bringing anything in, so I was paying the bills at home and taking care of us while he was getting more and more addicted to his new girlfriend; heroin. He helped out as far as bringing a lot of the traffic back through, but things were still not like they use to be at the barn. I was probably only making five-thousand dollars a month at the time. That wasn't much at all compared to what Dog was doing. He was getting to some real money around the county.

Uncle Ty came home in December. It didn't take much for him to get back into the swing of things. He still had his crew working the shop, the beach, and the bootlegger spots around Hallsboro. They had his money waiting for him as soon as he touched down. It was like he'd never left. It surprised him that heroin had my dad like it did, but it really didn't bother him too much. He knew Pop would get it together.

In the beginning of 93', this guy named Dent started coming around. Dent would come to cop from me, and somehow him and my dad got real cool. He was actually from Ashville, N.C, but he'd moved to Whiteville with his girlfriend. Dent was highly intelligent, he had a crack habit. You know, one of those college educated guys who was well-traveled and knowledgeable that just got out there on crack when the crack boom hit.

Dent and Pop would sit in the house and get high most of the time. Dent always had a few dollars. It took a little while to really figure out what he did for money. Dent was a white-collar crime guy. He would come up with credit card scams, write bad checks on other people's check books and whatever else he could do; a professional swindler. Him and my dad would ride out for a few hours and come back with a few thousand dollars from time-to-time. I loved it because Dent would always come spend his money with me. The amazing part about him was the fact that he knew a whole bunch of famous people. They would be sitting there watching television-getting high, and Dent would point someone out on television that he knew and always had an interesting story about them. I always used to mess with him and tell him he was lying, but he never let it bother him. He would just pick up the phone and call whoever it was that he was talking about. It was amazing because they really respected him and he was right here at my house getting high with my dad.

Around that time a lady from Whiteville named Cat used to come hang out with them. She'd been coming around since I was a little boy, but she was hanging heavy now that my mom had left. My dad and her didn't have anything going on, but she loved to get high. Her thing was sniffing cocaine. When she came over, you best believe she was going to treat her nose. She was a swindler to. Cat would always be trying to get some money out of one of Dent's hustles or connect my dad with people that would buy coke from him or sell it to him. She made a living being a middle man, and that chic was one of the greediest middle men I'd ever seen in my entire life. She was originally from New York City, very poised, well versed and personable. I always saw right through her though, most of us did, but she would fool a lot of people.

These three were a damn trip. They would get high and drink most of the time, but yet be plotting on how to get some money. That was their priority. As much as it hurt me to know that my dad was doing heroin, I noticed a little difference in him. He was getting back to wanting to make money.

Tragedy struck at Uncle Ty's shop and the barn. Uncle Ty and Spike left a fire burning in the small furnace in the shop while they went to get some supplies from Lake Waccamaw one day. When they got back, it was up in flames. Unc had been saying that the chimney needed to be cleaned for a few weeks, but hadn't gotten around to it because he was so busy. The shop burnt to the ground before the fire trucks had a chance to get there.

My granddaddy's brother, Ulysses, had come down from New Jersey and was staying in a camper that was beside the shop. Back in the day he would come down from Jersey to visit in nice Cadillac's, always had a different woman with him. He was pretty much an old pimp and decided to move down here when he got older. When the shop burned, the camper burned to. My dad ended up letting him move into the barn after the shop burned. He did a little cocaine every now-and-then, but he was cool.

Mont was always riding the go-cart that I bought him. One day he rode to the store and put gas in a kerosene jug. It was a youthful mistake. Ulysses was always doing small handy work around the barn to keep himself occupied. He didn't have a clue that gas was in the kerosene jug so he put some of it in the kerosene heater we had on the second floor of the barn. He didn't light it, but put it in there for the next person who decided to turn it on. The next person who wanted the heater on was Big Mike.

Big Mike had been getting high on that heroin all day and went to the barn to get some privacy. He really never liked to be bothered when he was getting high. It was kind of cold, and when he lit the heater, it burst into flames. Luckily I was up front in the house and noticed the smell of something burning. I ran out back to the barn and saw smoke coming from one of the second floor windows. I tried to get into it, but my dad had locked the door. My dad made his way to the door downstairs and tried to open it, but it was already piping hot. He got a serious burn from grabbing it and had to kick it open. We grabbed the water hose and were able to wet the outside walls down to prevent the fire from spreading, but it really wasn't under control until the fire department got there. It was damaged, but the damage wasn't too serious, just on the inside.

When the fire department and everyone else from around the way were out there, Big Mike was sitting down on the back porch of the house nodding out. That's when everyone got a good look at how bad Big Mike's problem was. That's the day my grandma figured it out.

"Petey, look at your dad over there nodding again. That man on something ain't he?" She said.

I just shook my head. My dad was a hot damn mess. Luckily, he was able to make it out of the barn. My grandma was thankful that he'd made it out ok, but I knew her. She was disappointed in him. She didn't know he was on heroin exactly, but she knew it was something. My grandfather sat down beside Pop. I don't know what they talked about, but it was serious. My dad looked at him while he sat there, but my grandfather never turned to face him. He said whatever it was he had to say, patted him on his shoulder and walked away. Whatever it was brought Pop out of all the nodding he was doing. Grandpa's talk bought him back to reality. My grandparents left right after. Most of the people from around the community who were there left right after.

My mom called the house that day after she'd heard what happened. She asked if Big Mike was ok, but when I asked her if she wanted to speak to him, she said no. She just wanted to make sure he was alright. They weren't together but she still loved him with all her heart. Nobody had to guess about that.

Uncle Ulysses apologized for putting the gas in the heater, but it wasn't his fault. It wasn't Mont's fault. It was just one of those things. GOD has a mysterious way of doing things. That day, He made Big Mike look at himself and see what he'd become. For the first time, he realized that heroin was ruining his life. That incident wasn't enough to make him stop, but it opened his eyes. Thank God.

Tim and I paid a few fiends that knew how to do carpentry work to help get the inside of the barn back together. The only thing we had to do was get the materials and give them a little cocaine. Big Mike helped out with paying and Tim and I helped them do the work. We needed that barn to stay up. That was our money maker.

A little while after then, not too many weeks later, Dent and my dad were in the house getting high as usual and Cat popped up. I guess she was having money problems, because she wasn't happy at all when she walked into the house. She was always flipping out when she had money problems. I was in the kitchen when she walked in, and overheard every word of her conversation with them from the time she walked through the door.

"Ya'll need to be ashamed of ya'll selves. Ya'll don't do nothing but get high all day, every damn day. Ya'll know all these dag gone people and act like ya'll forgot how to eat. What the hell is wrong with yall? Ya'll some smart damn dummies. If ya'll get yourselves together you can make some money, but this ain't goin' get it Mike. You better than this right here...." She said. She went on for about thirty minutes just telling them how sorry and lazy they were. I really didn't get it because she would come over all the time and get high with them. They were too high to even try to defend themselves.

She had been telling them about this guy that she knew up in New York that had it. He was one of the biggest hustlers in New York and was fronting people coke up and down the east coast. From my understanding, the only reason she'd never hooked them up was the fact that she thought they would mess up whatever dope he gave them. More than likely they would have because they were so busy getting high. I could understand, my dad wasn't the same Big Mike he used to be, and Dent hadn't been making matters any better. For whatever reason, more than likely it was greed, she called him that day. They didn't talk long and when she got off the phone, she told them that he was coming down soon.

He got there a few days later. His name was Raz. Raz wasn't a flashy guy, but he was a real clean cut dude. When he came down, he went to Cat's house and they came over. He and my dad knew a lot of the same people, and he and Dent had some mutual associates as well. He'd heard about both of them, and I guess he felt comfortable because before he left the house, he left them with a half kilo of cocaine.

With me hustling out of the barn, Uncle Ty and Dog doing their thing; it didn't take long at all for that half a bird to get gone. Big Mike didn't give us anything, but he sold it to us cheaper than we were able to get it from anywhere else-significantly cheaper.

Raz would show up every couple of weeks, collect his money and leave those two with more coke. Each time he came the packages got bigger. I guess he started them out with a half kilo to see what they would do with it. Within a few months Raz was leaving them one or two kilos a month. Big Mike wouldn't hustle too tough around Hallsboro other than selling me, Dog and Uncle Ty what we needed. He and Dent would hit the highway and get most of it off. They would make a lot of trips to Greenville, N.C, Charlotte, Greensboro, and other major cities around North Carolina. They would split a few thousand dollars, but their habits didn't slow down any so it was almost like they were working for pennies.

Dog and Uncle Ty were copping dope from other places to, but they would still cop from Pop because the dope Raz was giving them was so good. The traffic at the barn was growing fast. The fiends loved that cocaine. Tim was still working, but finally, some real money was coming through the barn again. I kept telling him that he was going to have to quit his job because I really needed his help. I wasn't getting a wink of sleep, and I even tried to go to Southeastern Community College, like I said I was going to do, but I didn't have time for school; that didn't last long. I was a full time hustler.

Uncle Ty was taking the money he was making from the coke game and investing in buying cars for his lot. It was the smart thing to do, because it showed that he had an income coming in from a legal means. You would have thought that he would have slowed down selling coke when his car business was making good money, but Unc wasn't like that. He'd been hustling since a teenager and absolutely nothing was going to make him give it up or slow down. The coke money was too good to slow down.

Dog was doing better than he'd ever done. His team in Whiteville was making a killing, but it was high risk over there. See, we only had to worry about sheriff patrols coming through every now and again. The city of Whiteville had a large police force. Dog and his team over there had to worry about them and sheriff deputies. Whiteville was hot as hell.

Raz loved Dent and Pop because they always had his money when he came down, and they didn't take long getting the work off. Think about it, they both needed money to support their habits so they weren't trying to mess that up. Nobody ever spoke to Raz except those two. That was their business, so no one ever needed to meet him. I would see him pull up to the house. Sometimes Cat would even be with him, but there wasn't a need to meet him.

CHAPTER 12 – WISE, BUT NOT SMART

Dawana was just happy to have me around. She was a senior in high school and working, so other than the weekends, there wasn't a whole lot of time to see her anyway. By this time her mom caught a whiff of what I was doing so she didn't like me at all. Sometimes I would call there for Dawana, and if her mom would pick up the phone, she would just hang up on me. She never told Dawana why she didn't like me, but she told her to stay away from me. That was hard for her to deal with. She loved me and saw a future for me and her. Every girl wants her mom to like the man she sees in her future. This wasn't the case by a long shot. Most times we saw each other, she had to sneak away to see me. It wasn't a lot, but that worked out great because I was hustling anyway. It also made it easier for me to do my thing with other women. That never slowed down. I would have women come through the barn all times of the night-always.

When 94' came around, all of us were doing well. That year was when the traffic in Hallsboro was just getting going good again. Uncle Ty always did great, but by now, me and Tim were playing with some real cash. Tim quit his job that year. He was making ten times more money hustling at the barn, so there wasn't a need for him to keep working. Dog was doing his thing in Whiteville, but he started getting a slew of petty charges. He never got caught with coke, but he loved smoking weed. He would always get caught with marijuana riding in his car. Nothing big at all, but every few months he would get caught with a half-ounce or something smaller. That's what he kept on him to smoke. A weed charge wasn't that big of a deal, but he was already on probation. If he violated his probation, he would have to do some time. He was playing with fire.

My dad's heroin addiction was still there, but it wasn't. Let me explain...

Big Mike started traveling like he used to when him and Dent met Raz. Because of all that traveling and trying to move the coke he was getting, he really didn't have a whole lot of time to sit still too long. When he was sitting still, you best believe that he was putting heroin in his nose, but other than that; he was trying to move cocaine again. Staying busy was actually helping a little. He just wasn't staying busy doing the right things.

My homeboy 'Killer', one of the Hooptie Crew, was going to college at Elizabeth City State College at the time. He would come home to Hallsboro on the weekends and get to see how we were getting down. The college life, especially when you don't have a job while you're going to school, can be tough. Killer didn't want to get a job because his school work load was already enough, but he wanted to make some money. Uncle Ty ended up fronting him a few pounds of weed to take to school with him. I don't know how he did it, but he started making a killing on that campus. Those college kids were smoking weed like the fiends in Hallsboro were smoking crack. Killer started out a little slow, but as the word grew on campus, he started making some serious money. Ty always talked about how much money Killer was making in school. It blew his mind that those college kids were smoking that much reefer. By now, almost all of my boys from Hallsboro were drug dealers. Not small timers, we were all getting to some serious cash. We would have never guessed that 'Killer' would become a preacher years later.

Everything was going good for everybody, almost too good. Then, something happened again. Mike and Dent were doing their thing. Mike was responsible for most of what was happening, but Dent played a big role too. He was connecting Big Mike with a lot of hustlers he knew around North and South Carolina. At any rate, they were good as long as Raz came when he said he was going to come to get his money. I don't know what happened with Raz this one time, but he didn't show up for a month. Cat couldn't get up with him, and he wasn't answering Big Mike and Dent's call. They didn't know if he got locked up, murdered, or what. Then out the blue, he called and said he was going to be there in a week. You gotta understand, Mike and Dent's habit didn't just stop. The guys were still getting high. If both of them were just doing cocaine, everything would have been fine. That wasn't the case. Pop's heroin habit was expensive, real expensive. An ounce of cocaine was around seven hundred fifty dollars, versus an ounce of heroin costing around five-thousand dollars. When they didn't have coke to get rid of, they were sitting still. When they were sitting still, they were using. Basically, it wasn't good for them boys to sit still too long. When Raz didn't show up for that extended period, that gave them just enough rope to hang themselves.

One day I was in the barn serving as usual, and Dent came back there. It had been a good day for me, so I thought he was coming to cop from me. There were a few people in there waiting on me to serve them, but Dent told me he needed to holla at me about something really important. Right after I finished with the fiends who were in there, I spoke with him. He looked like something was really wrong, so I thought he had some bad news about my Pop or something like that.

"Pete, I ain't goin lie to you and you know I ain't the type that's going to ever let my pride get in the way. Raz ain't showed up man, and we been waiting on this fool for over a month. Me and Mike done messed up the damn money and now he coming down. It ain't nobody else

problem but ours, but Mike ain't trying to figure nothing out. He in there high right now, and we about ten thousand dollars short on that damn money!!!" Dent said that and before I could respond, Big Mike came through the door. Dent motioned for me not to say anything, so I acted like we were talking about something else. I can't remember what it was, but it worked. Big Mike didn't have a clue of what we were talking about.

Later that night Dent came back to the barn again to speak with me. This time, he had a proposition. He told me that they had a couple ounces left and that he needed me to break them down and sell them. Then he wanted to borrow the rest of the money. Long story short, they needed about six grand and for me to break down and sell the two or three ounces they had left. In return, he was going to pay me back my six grand, and give me a big 8 (four and a half ounces) when Raz came. Supposedly Raz was supposed to be giving them five kilos this time around. If they didn't have his money, heaven knows what was going to happen. Getting those five kilos would be a beautiful thing all the way around. Not having Raz's bread, well, that would have been disastrous.

Dent didn't know when Raz was coming, but even if he would have came that same night I would had those two or three ounces sold, traffic was moving real good. The six grand definitely wasn't a problem. It didn't take long for me to think, I jumped on it. I couldn't go wrong with getting a big 8 and my money back. The only thing I had an issue with was giving Dent and my Dad the money without being able to meet with Raz. I told Dent I would give him the money whenever Raz came.

Raz came over within the next few days. I was in my room on the phone with Dawana when he came in. Dent and Big Mike were in the living room-high as usual. I hurried and got off the phone with her because I knew I had to give Dent the money. I already had it ready, ten- thousand dollars. I don't know what the full amount was that they owed him, but that part wasn't my business. I was about to walk out into the living room, but something told me to stand by my bedroom door for a second and listen to what was going on; I'm glad I did.

I couldn't make out the words they exchanged in the beginning, but after I stood there for a few seconds they got louder. Raz was the one raising his voice...

"Why ya'll clowns playing with my money?!?! I treat you like gentlemen, give you my coke to help ya'll broke-fiend-asses out and you spit in my face. The only reason I come down here is for you and look at what I get. Ya'll sniffing my sh#t, and Big Mike look at you. You two ain't worth a bag of horse sh#$! Right now..."

I couldn't believe what I was hearing, and aside from that, I couldn't believe my dad and Dent didn't say a word back. I was pissed the hell off, and before I knew it I'd put one of my pistols in my pants and burst out of the room screaming on this dude.

"Bruh, who the hell you talking to? You come in my damn house screaming and disrespecting like you actually mean sh*# in here. You don't come in nobody crib doing that. That's how stupid asses get their brains blown out, like you ain't had no home training or nothing...."

My dad and Dent stood there staring at what was happening with their eyes wide open. They couldn't believe I was talking to him like that, but I didn't care. He was disrespecting my house. I called it my house because I was the one paying the bills and keeping food in the refrigerator.

"I got the rest of yo' damn money but you the dumb ass for leaving them with a package that long any way, knowing both of them get high. You stupid as hell for not showing up when you was supposed to! What the fu#$ you thought was goin happen?!?! Take this damn money bruh and get the f@#k out before something bad happen to you today."

I reached in my pocket, pulled out the ten grand, and threw it on the coffee table in front of the couch. Dent stood up and reiterated everything I'd just said.

"You know you took too long to come back. We sold that little bit of shi# you gave us right after you put it in our hands. You know we get high..." He saw how hot I was, so he just joined in with me. My dad joined right along as well.

"Raz you know you wrong for coming up in here disrespecting my house man. We ain't that cool for you to be talking to us any ole type of way."

I could tell by looking at Raz that he was scared. He quickly apologized, but I wasn't in the mood to hear nothing.

"Forgive me brother, you must be Petey? I got a little upset, but you would too if the shoe was on the other foot. My sincere apologies, I was wrong. They told me a lot about you. I'll tell you what, what you need? I'll front you something real nice and we can let bygones be bygones."

I was in my feelings by then. I didn't want anything from him, and I couldn't help but shake my head before I responded. Dent was standing behind him with his head tilted in the air and his thumbs in the air. He wanted me to take whatever Raz was going to give me. My father on the other hand looked at me with a blank face. He'd always let me make my own decisions, and he was letting me handle this one on my own.

"Man I don't want nothing from you. I'll pay for whatever I get. If you want to give me something, that's cool, but I don't want no front bruh." I was stern-meant everything I said. In that moment, Raz was impressed by what he was seeing. It was written all over his face.

My dad and Dent owed me six grand and a big eight right then, so they had to get the five kilos that Raz was going to give them originally. I had close to five grand I could spend after I'd given Dent and my dad the money to pay Raz. Raz told me that if I gave him five thousand, he could give me a quarter kilo and a big 8. That was the sweetest deal I'd ever seen in the dope game. I was getting thirteen and a half ounces of coke for five grand. I was making close to twenty-five hundred dollars an ounce back then, so you do the math. I was going to make over thirty-three thousand dollars, plus my Father and Dent owed me six grand and a big 8. Give or take, if Raz was still going to give Dent and my dad the five kilos and they paid me back, I was going to net a little over fifty thousand dollars at the end of the day.

Raz was a little reluctant, but my dad and Dent had never messed up until then. He ended up giving them the five kilos and gave me what he promised me for five-thousand. That's the night I started playing ball with the big boys...

Later on that night when I saw Dog and told him what happened, his mind was blown. Of course he wanted to meet up with

Raz the next time he came down. Uncle Ty always got coke from a few different people. He had connects all over the place, but he wanted to meet with Raz as well. The fiends loved that particular dope. That's one thing they knew about my dad, even from the early days, he always had the best coke.

Things started changing real fast for me. I had enough coke to sell to the small time hustlers around the area. That's the traffic I wanted. Tim and I started putting the word out that I could serve anything less than an ounce. They started coming quicker than we'd expected. It's a good thing Raz was coming right back the very next week.

Dent and my Dad were on the road as usual, and the barn was wide open. They paid me back right before Raz came again, and gave me the big 8 like they'd promised. When Raz came, Dog and I put our money together and bought a kilo. From that moment forward, I knew I was never going to turn back.

It was good to see that my dad wasn't sitting around snorting heroin all day. He didn't completely stop right then either, but it didn't have the same hold on him that it had before. Around that time he kept talking to Dent and Spike about opening the El Derado back up. Spike was all for it, but there was one problem. Dent and Pop were traveling around so much. That's why my dad closed the club before; he was too busy hustling and didn't have the time to run it like it needed to be ran. The topic would come up more often as the year went by.

Dawana graduated high school that year. She was either the Valedictorian or salutatorian, I can't remember, but all her hard work had paid off. All of her family was at her graduation, so when I came, I sat away from them. I figured her mom still didn't take too kindly to me. The second the graduation was over she ran straight over to me and hugged me like I was the only person on the planet. She was set to head for college in August at UNCW. It was close to home and with her being there, we would be able to spend a lot more time together; away from everybody. I was proud of who she became and what she was becoming. She was my normalcy and my refuge from the chaotic drug scene.

...But, on my birthday that year, Me, Dog, Skeeter Rock, and Juice went to this spot called the GFB club in Ashe. It was an after-hours spot that was always packed-so many beautiful women to choose from. We spent out in that club that night.

I saw 'her' as soon as I walked in the club. She was dark, classy, 5'2, and had the prettiest smile I'd ever seen at that point. Her body was just amazing. She was warm to my eyes, and by far, was the finest woman that was in that building that night. When I approached her, she had this inviting personality. Her name was Tootie. I felt her from Jump Street. She was engaging, intelligent and going to school at NC State - I wanted her.

I had on a fly outfit. I always had on something fly, but my birthdays were extra fly for me. We drank top shelf, pop bottles all night, and bought the bar out wherever it was for sale- ninety percent of the times we went out. She noticed me early in the night.

Me and the boys walked outside to smoke some weed, it was almost time for the club to close anyway. In passing her, I told her I was about to leave. She was talking with a group of girls, so I didn't want to interrupt her conversation. I just told her and kept moving. She told me to give her second, but she was taking too long. We had to be out there in front of the club for at least twenty minutes. She didn't come so we hopped in the car and pulled off. Pulling out of the parking lot, Dog noticed her coming out of the club and looking around. It was just by chance that he noticed her because he was looking through the passenger side view mirror when he saw her. I turned around immediately and pulled up to her.

Now, she talked trash about me not waiting on her, but it was cool. She gave me her number. I gave her my pager number, that's when pagers were the 'it' thing. She paged me the very next morning and invited me to her family reunion that day. It threw me by surprise, but she was fine; we had to go- Me, Skeeter Rock and Juice. We had an incredible time, her family was really cool.

She was spontaneous, so I had to show her my spontaneous side. She was leaving to go back to school with one of her home girls, Dee, that Sunday. I told her me and a few of my dudes were going to come to Raleigh and get some rooms for the week. She was blown away, but extremely intrigued. It was all over her face, I mean, she couldn't hide it. Low and behold, when they were leaving to go to school...Me, my homeboy Derrick, Juice, and Skeeter Rock met them at her mom's house to follow them up.

That week was off the chain. We partied with them for about three days and then it was back to the trap. I always felt bad when I cheated on Dawana, but this time wasn't like that. Tootie was the beautiful taste of something new.

That weekend, I was in Whiteville handling some business and I got a page from the pay phone at Time Savers, a gas station. I knew it was that payphone because people who wanted work had paged me from that phone all the time. I didn't call back right away, but after a minute or two, they were paging me again. When I called, she picked up. She wanted to surprise me, and knew White-ville was next to Hallsboro, so she called from there. I came up to the Time Saver, and she was looking like a million dollars standing next to her car. She ended up staying in Hallsboro that whole week. She knew I had a girlfriend, she knew I hustled, and she didn't care. She didn't condone any of it, but we connected so well that it really didn't matter. I felt like she was well worth the risk of getting caught.

I had two bad chics at the same damn time...

Each time Raz came, he had to bring more cocaine. My dad was buying his own work again, Me and Dog was copping together, and Uncle Ty was copping.

Eventually something always happens. Everything we do in life has consequences, good or bad. The consequences of Dog getting caught with weed came when no one ever expected. He got caught again in Whiteville. This time, he was sentenced to four months in prison for violating probation.

While he was away, I handled his work. The traffic at the barn grew, and when the news got around that Dog was locked up, it grew even more. A lot of the hustlers and fiends that were going to Dog started showing up.

Raz came a few more times, but kept telling us that he was going to chill out on all that driving and send someone. He wouldn't tell us who he was sending but he always laughed and told us that we'd know. It got around that time that he was supposed to come down and we got a call from him telling us that someone would be coming to see us the next day. He usually called a day or two before he came so we could get our money ready. Now that was a dangerous thing for someone in his line of work to do, because someone could have had someone waiting to rob him, or the police waiting on him when he got there, but we were like family at the point. He trusted us, we trusted him.

Me and Tim were out in the barn the next evening serving like we always did, and Mont walked in and told us that an old white lady was outside taking stuff out of her trunk in the driveway. Me and Tim hurried out to see what was going on, and there was this old white station wagon out there. When we walked up to see who it was, there was this older white lady at the trunk. I asked her who she was, and before she could respond, we saw that she had a trunk full of pears, apples, and some other fruits and vegetables. She also had a few cases of jars. I figured she was trying to sell us some produce.

"Hey guys I'm Sally," and kept messing with stuff in her trunk. Tim and I just kind of looked at each other.

"Ok, mam we don't want any of what you selling. We preciate you stopping by though." Tim said. She stopped what she was doing and turned around towards us wiping her hands off. It was a weird moment. This lady had to be in her mid-60's or early-70's.

"I'm sorry, I forgot to ask you. Is Big Mike here? My buddy Raz sent me over here to see him."

By that time, Pop had walked outside. *"Oh, there you are my friend."* She said, as she walked over towards him. They hugged and chatted like they'd been friends for years. Me and Tim put two and two together and came to the conclusion that Raz had sent this old white woman.

They went inside the house. Me and Tim walked in a few minutes later and when we did, Big Mike was counting a lot of money sitting on the couch. She was sitting at the other end of it. I asked Pop what was up and he told me to go get my money together and page Ty. Sally had the work. She'd actually been to our house before, I wasn't around.

She was energetic for her age; small framed Jewish lady that looked like one of those ladies that worked as a greeter at Wal Mart, a real golden girl. Tim and I went up the road to grab the cash and paged Ty when we got back.

"Pete, Raz got to be one of the smartest people in the country. Man he got this old lady driving bricks up and down the road!!! This like something off a damn movie cousin. Raz ain't no joke." Tim said.

While we were in the barn, Big Mike and Sally came outside and sat on the porch. By then Uncle Ty pulled up. He walked up on the porch and Pop introduced them. When Tim and I got our money together and gave it to her, she put it in the big purse she had with her and told us that she would be back shortly. Raz was a straight up guy, so we really didn't have a problem with her getting our money and coming back. The big question was...when exactly was she coming back?

It took her about an hour, but she came right back. Sally had left the work in the hotel she was staying in Whiteville. I guess she was being cautious. When she came back, she had our order in a suitcase in the back seat. We helped her get the suitcase and when she got inside, she served all of us one-by-one. It was a little late so she left and went to the hotel, but we would see a lot more of her over the next few years-a whole lot more of her.

CHAPTER 13 – TOO DEEP

I would go visit Dawana often while she was at school, but Tootie was growing on me. As time went by I started spending more time with her. She would come to the house mostly. Shallotte wasn't that far away so it was easy for her to come into town to see me and then drop by to see her family there. A few months after we'd met, her parents separated. It was a devastating time for her. She'd grown up in a somewhat Cosby Show-like situation and all of a sudden things turned for the worse. At that point, from my understanding, that was the toughest thing she'd ever had to deal with. Depression is mutha. It's the kind of thing that turns hustlers into dope fiends and college students with 4.0 GPA's into college drop outs. For her, dropping out was a necessity. It was too hard to concentrate on her studies while her heart constantly cried for her parents. She moved back home and started spending a lot more time in Hallsboro. I was so in love with her, I didn't mind at all. My family and circle became her pseudo-family. I would have never guessed it, but her and my father would eventually become the best of friends.

With coke traffic continuing to grow in Hallsboro, everybody was busier than they'd ever been. My love for Dawana was still very much alive, but with Tootie being around so much I was slowly, but surely, falling in love with her. My heart didn't stop loving Dawana, but I was undoubtedly in love Tootie as well. The perfect storm was brewing right under my nose. I guess I was too focused on the coke business to notice.

Eventually, Big Mike acted on all the talking he was doing about opening the El Derado back up. This time he wanted to really focus on it and turn it into a thriving establishment. My father was a master marketer. He didn't need television or radio ads, a public relations person, or even fliers. The only thing he used was what he was blessed with; his mouth. When Pop put the word out about anything, whether it was drugs or anything, people listened and the word would spread like wild fire. On the opening night, it seemed like Michael Jackson was doing a free concert in Bolton. It had to be over five-hundred people there that night. After the building was packed to capacity, the party overflowed into the parking lot and the street. You would think that it would have subsided after a while, nah. It was like that every night he opened the doors; four nights a week.

Uncle Ty and Big Mike always did things unorthodox. See nowadays people fight and cut up in little spots in rural areas-it wasn't like that at the El Derado. For one, people knew not to act up over there because of our reputation. We were tagged 'infamous and notorious'. For two, Unc and Pop had a set of boxing gloves in there. If a fight broke out, they would round up the two fools who were fighting, make them put on the boxing gloves, and fight right there in the middle of the dance floor. If they didn't want to fight then, then of course both of them would get their asses kicked by so many people it was crazy. After that beating they would be tossed out in the street, and the party would go on. That was the perfect system, because there weren't over two fights in that club as long as it stayed open, and all the other clubs in the area had fights and shootings almost every weekend.

The El Derado was a hot club, but you know what was going on there. Hustlers came from near and far to do business with us. If you wanted a dime bag of weed, you could get it. If you wanted a kilo of cocaine, well, you could get that too. The club was making great money, but that little building couldn't compete with the dope sales that were generated there a week.

Here's how it worked...

Hustlers would come to the club to cop and party with the most beautiful women in the area. That goes hand-in-hand; beautiful women and money. Then, the same hustlers and fiends that came to the club would start coming through Hallsboro when the club wasn't open. With the popularity of the club, came more clientele.

The clientele always grew; therefore the traffic coming through Hallsboro always grew at a rapid pace. The methodology seemed simple enough. I don't think anyone knew that it was going to happen like that, but who ever really knows what's going to happen in life. I don't think Pop masterminded it the way the Feds claimed he did. It just kind of happened.

Sally would come every week or so. By this time, she was bringing over ten kilos a trip. It always amazed us that this little old white Jewish lady was riding that coke up and down the highway. When she came to bring us work, she would usually spend a night or two recuperating from all the driving she was doing. She would relax; do some cross stitching, or canned fruits and vegetables. Sally was dropping off kilos to us, down in Atlanta, out in Alabama-all over the place. Raz's operation spread across multiple states. It was nothing for her to be traveling with a few hundred thousand dollars. She had nerves of steel. Anybody could have easily robbed her, but she was such a sweet old lady; the thought of it probably never crossed their mind. Sometimes, she would stay a few days, she loved being in the country.

I was watching my dad slowly come off of heroin. Socializing more, because of the club, and traveling again was therapeutic in a sense. When Tootie would come, her and him would sit up and talk for hours. I hadn't heard my dad laugh like that and be in such a good mood in years. It went from me walking into the house or the barn seeing him nodding out on heroin, to me walking in and seeing him watching a movie or chit chatting with Tootie. Those two loved each other; it made me a little jealous. LOL

One of the closest people in my life, my grandma, noticed that I was driving Tootie's car all the time. She hadn't met Tootie yet. I didn't think that would be a good idea. Grandma loved Dawana. It was a red Nissan Maxima, almost brand new. I was still stopping by my grandparent's frequently either to grab something to eat or just sit and talk.

"Baby, why you always driving that red car? Who's car is that Petey?" She would ask. I always blew it off at first and went to another subject, but she wouldn't stop asking. That car made her curious.

"You know, you and Dawana been together so long. I love that girl. Baby I don't know what you doing, but please, please, don't mess up a good thing over nothing crazy." She said.

Grandma always gave it to me straight. Hell, she gave it to everybody straight. Some of the older ladies in the community, her friends, would always have something to say about what we were doing. She hated what we did, she was no fool, but she loved us all the same.

She would tell them things like ***"Y'all talk about my boys selling dope, but yo kids the ones buying it. They ain't no better..."*** She would preach to us, like every good mother or grandmother would, telling us to stop. At that point, it was easier said than done. She was a deeply devoted Christian lady, and a realist. She knew that we were too deep in the game to just walk away overnight. She wanted us to, but it just wasn't that easy.

A few guys started hanging around during that time. This white guy named M.Green would come often. He was a big weed dealer out back in Riegelwood. He was getting his weed from Uncle Ty, but would come down and hang at the barn with us. He was around our age, making a little bit of money, and just a cool cat. There was also this guy named Pogie from East Arcadia. Pogie used to sell coke real heavy a few years prior. I forget why he'd stopped. Maybe he got locked up or something, but he was one of those names that was buzzing years before. He started coming to the club talking to me, Tim, and Juice. He was only a few years older than us. That turned into him and his cousin Stretch coming to hang out with us at the barn. Everybody was coming by the barn then. Most of those people were fiends and hustlers coming by to cop, but there was a few people that came to kick it with us.

Around then there was a drought. It was hard as hell for a lot of people to find dope, and even if they did find it, the prices had sky rocketed for a spell. We were good because we had so much of it, but our connect even started feeling the pinch after a while. Raz came himself a time or two instead of sending Sally. That's when we found out exactly what his story was.

Raz asked me to borrow some money one day. Now that's strange in and of itself. Connects don't ever borrow money from who they're selling to. But he was like family so when he explained, it all made sense.

Right before Cat introduced us to Raz, something monumental happened. He'd been copping dope from a Dominican lady in New York for years. Over those years they developed a close friendship. As to how close, I don't know, but they were very close from what he explained.

At any rate, she got caught up in some big coke conspiracy in New York. When she got locked up, Raz knew exactly where her stash spot was and had access to it. She was given over twenty years in the federal penitentiary, so the work she had was of no use to her. The thing about it, when she got locked up she had almost three-hundred kilos. Raz worked it.

Raz was a business man with expensive taste. You would have never been able to guess from the way he looked when he came down, but that's what he was. What happened was he bought a home worth over a million dollars in the Poconos and started a gym in some part of New York. That was over a five-hundred thousand dollar investment. He still had some of the work left, but he was getting close to the end. When that happened he found a new connect. However, the price of coke was so damn high during the drought, and he had a ton of money tied up.

We knew something was up, because he went from being able to bring us ten kilos at a time, to only being able to bring about four. He asked for a hundred grand because he was meeting his connect soon. He was like family, but this is the dope game. You can't just go around trusting everybody. I don't know why he came to me instead of going to Big Mike or Uncle Ty, maybe it was his pride, but I let him hold sixty-thousand. He asked me whether or not I wanted the loan back in money or coke. That wasn't a hard decision to make at all, I wanted the coke. A few weeks later, he came down with the repayment- three kilos of cocaine. Considering what the price of coke was right then, I'd made off real nice.

That was right around the time that Dog came home, so it was lovely. I'd been turning Dog's package since he'd been locked up so his money was tied into mine. It blew his mind that I was able to buy four or five kilos at a time. The progress we'd made while he was in prison was out of this world. I gave him two keys, and he was right back in business. Only this time around, he had a whole lot more coke. His team never stopped and eagerly awaited his return. It blew their minds too when he stepped back on the scene with so much work. Things were going great for everybody again.

That summer was crazy. You know, things can be going so great in life and you just feel like something bad is going to happen. I didn't know what it was, but I felt it. I always thought about getting shot, murdered, locked up, or whatever-that's just the nature of the game. My feeling was right, but I was wrong about thinking it had anything to do with my coke endeavors.

Dawana was out of school and living back at her mom's for the summer. She never left her job at the jewelry store, so she just picked up hours there when she was home. She was still oblivious to the fact I was hustling, I was still doing an impeccable job of keeping that away from her. On Saturday mornings before she went to work, we had this thing. There was this little country diner that sat almost right in the middle of Hallsboro and Lake Waccamaw. That's where her mom's house was, Lake Waccamaw. She would stop by there and pick us up breakfast every Saturday morning and bring it by the house; fish, grits and eggs.

Well on this particular morning my cousin had come over to wash my car. I'd been out all night partying with Tootie at the El Derado and got a lil drunk, so my mind wasn't running on all its cylinders anyway. The bad thing about it was, Tootie spent the night. Maybe she stayed because she wanted to make sure I was ok, or maybe she was a little tipsy, I don't know, but I do know I was dead wrong.

My cousin left out to run to the store to get some tire shine, and as fate would have it-this nut left the front door unlocked.

So what did Dawana do? She pulls up and comes to the front door. After a few knocks and no answer, she turned the knob and walked in. It wasn't anything unusual for her to do. Most times Big Mike and Mont would be gone. I would wake up early on occasion and call her to tell her that I would leave the door open for her. Uncle Ulysses would be up and moving around the barn, so I never really worried about someone coming up into the house without being noticed. As soon as she walked in, I was awaken by her voice. Dawana was a sweetheart, and would always be bright-eyed and bushy-tailed in the morning.

"Peeeetey...Wake up baby I'm running late." She said, as I heard her heels on the hardwood floor getting closer to my room door. Tootie and I had fallen asleep listening to soft music from an R&B station we were able to find on the radio, but her voice was loud enough to carry over the soft music. It all happened in a split second. I woke up, heard those heels getting closer, and hopped out the bed and darted to my room door just as she opened it.

Tootie and I were fully clothed, so that was a plus, but whatever song was playing then didn't help the situation at all. It was a slow song, so lying and saying Tootie was just a friend was out of the question. I wasn't able to push the door back closed until it opened about half way.

*"**Baby give me a second**"* I blurted, but it was too late. She'd already seen Tootie lying on the bed before I had a chance to push the door all the way back. The breakfast plate she had for me dropped to the floor. Simultaneously she took in a deep breath in awe of what she'd just seen.

She immediately started crying while she tried to ask - *"**Petey what did I do to you?!?!**"* Before I could answer her standing behind that door thinking this was the worst day of my life, I heard those heels running back down the hallway and the front door being slammed shut. When that door slammed, I cringed and slowly turned around towards my bed. Tootie was sitting up by now, with a 'what-just-happened' look on her face.

Since middle school, Dawana had been my princess. No matter how many women I'd slept with, she was my heart-my 'normal' in the crazy life I was living. She loved me more that any benevolent term could describe, and in one moment, my immature care of her heart ruined what we built for so long.

That was when I realized that I'd become everything that I hated about my dad when I was growing up. I was the man that I promised myself I'd never be.

What I was experiencing in that room, at that particular moment in time, was bitter sweet. On one hand, I'd lost the love of my life. On the other hand I was looking at a new love that was exhilarating and pleasing to all my senses, to say the least.

We didn't have to talk about what just happened, it was what it was. As I looked into her eyes and we gazed at each other, I realized that I wasn't afraid of falling in love with her.

CHAPTER 14 - EXPANSION

Tootie was always outspoken, even in her childhood from what I've heard. The mix of emotions she was going through because of her parent's separation gave her fuel to be even more outspoken. For whatever reason it was, she couldn't take any more of the hurt that staying in her parent's house was causing her. There were so many memories of growing up as a happy family. She ended up moving in with us. Her and my dad, and the rest of my family, would become even closer.

Raz and his new connect were doing good business. The coke was a little high, but that was to be expected during the drought. They were good, but Raz had bigger fish to fry. Even though the Dominican lady, who left him with all that cocaine, had a ton of time to serve, that didn't equate to her not wanting her money. Her son bumped into Raz walking down the street in Queens and had a very serious conversation with him. Pretty much, he wanted the money. I don't know what the details are, but Raz seemed like he was scared for his life when he asked me to borrow more money. This time, he wanted to borrow sixty-thousand. I let him get the money, but I was focused on finding a new connect after then. Raz started having too much going on for my taste.

Pogie and his cousin Stretch started coming around a lot more, to the barn and the club. He would always bring up the fact that he had a connect in Raleigh that was selling kilos for nineteen-thousand. Compared to the price we were getting them for, it was incredible; especially in the drought. We always listened, but told him we didn't want to do anything because our connect was doing us right. He was cool, but you know, you don't just do business with anybody.

He pressed us for about two months talking about the connect he knew in Raleigh. In the meantime, Sally was telling us about an issue she had with Raz. She told us that Raz was paying her fifteen hundred dollars a kilo to deliver, but over those past few months, he got behind on paying her. She was making a ton of money, but she had grandkids she was taking care of and a ton of bills between the two houses she owned. One was in Florida, the other in New York. The lady was doing a good job; she needed her money. Plus, she was such a sweet old lady. We couldn't figure out why Raz wasn't doing her right. That was more reason for me to search out a new connect.

Tim and I decided to see what Pogie was talking about. The next time him and Stretch came to the club, we told them to stop by the barn whenever they had time. They showed up the very next day. We didn't want to buy a whole kilo. We decided to buy a half, just to see if everything was like he said. We gave them ten thousand dollars and they set sail for Raleigh. They were supposed to be back that next morning, but never showed. We really didn't worry too much, it was only ten thousand dollars, and then we got the news...

The story we got was that they went to the connect, just like they were supposed to, and picked up the work. On their way out of the particular area that they picked the work up from, they stopped to get gas and grab something to eat from a service station. Stretch walked in to pay for the gas while Pogie went inside to grab something to eat. After Stretch pumped the gas, he pulled into a parking space beside the station, close to the door. The guy that he copped the work from rolled into the gas station with three guys in his car. They pulled next to Stretch and robbed him of the work that they just bought. The side of the station that they were parked was dimly lit and there weren't many people there. When Pogie came out of the gas station, one of the guys shot him in the head as he walked out of the door. Pogie died on the spot. Stretch suffered injury from being pistol whipped, but his life was spared. The guys sped off, never to be caught. I would find out what really happened years later right before I was released from the feds...

Tim and I were out of ten thousand dollars, but that didn't really hurt us. The heart wrenching part was the fact that another young man lost his life to the street. Everyone knows that in the street you end up either dead or in jail if you stay out there, but the truth is, it's better to go see someone locked up, than to see them getting buried. There are tons of mothers out there that wish they could go see their sons in prison, versus going to visit their son's gravesite...

Right around then, the white guy, M.Green, who was buying all that weed from Uncle Ty, was trying his hand at selling cocaine. Multiple people that bought weed from him would ask him if he could get his hands on any coke, and he kept telling them that he was going to get some. He started off buying from my dad, then he started buying from me, my dad, and Tim. His business was growing faster than he expected. M.Green was making a name for himself.

With Tootie living with us and me and her being together day-for-day, it was bound to happen, and it did-she got pregnant. The first person I told was Uncle Ulysses. The news made him happier than I'd seen him in is older days. The second person I told was my grandma. She was happy, but even more surprised. Grandma really didn't come to the house a lot around then. There was way too much traffic coming through to have her come down there. Those few months that Tootie had been there, Grandma didn't know anything about her. The only thing she knew was that I had been driving that red car.

Big Mike found out from Tootie. They had that type of close-knit relationship. He and I had a real talk the day he found out. It wasn't like the father-son talks you see on television, but it was good enough for me. He really put it in my head that I should be a good father and not make the same mistakes that he'd made.

As far as my grandparents...When I introduced Tootie to my grandma, they hit it off right away. My grandma was tickled at the fact that she knew I was dealing with someone other than Dawana because of that car I was driving, but she was happy to be bringing a great grandchild into the world. Their relationship became tighter than Tootie and my Pop's. Within a few short months, those two were inseparable.

I noticed some big changes in my father. That lost look in his eyes that he had when he would be out there on heroin wasn't there anymore. He had a whole lot more energy. Instead of sitting up all day with just Dent, he was getting out of the house more to socialize with his friends. Dent would still go with him when he was taking coke out of town, but they didn't do a lot of hanging together as tough as they used to. Big Mike was back to his old self. He'd actually quit heroin under our noses.

With Tootie being pregnant, I didn't want her to be around the house like that. She spent a lot of time with my grandmother. They were BFF's, but I couldn't imagine raising a child in that environment. We started looking for a home, away from Hallsboro. I was twenty-one years old with a few hundred thousand dollars cash and a few hundred thousand dollars worth of cocaine. We could have moved anywhere that we wanted to. What better place to move than Shallotte. We would be close to her parents, and only about thirty minutes from Hallsboro. We bought a home right beside the house she grew up in. Her mother still lived there, so it worked out perfectly on every level.

The money I spent buying the house was just a small dent in my wallet. Things were going so good at that point; I made it back in less than two months. It was the perfect move, and it allowed me to be somewhat elusive. I spent most of my time there. When I would leave the barn, nobody really knew where I was going other than Tim, Dog, Uncle Ty and a few others in my immediate circle. That move would turn out to be a great one after all. I would find out later that it made it even harder for federal agents to keep up with me.

Me, Dog, Tim, and Juice would go to the mall and a lot of the clothing stores around the area, and spend a few thousand dollars on clothes. It wasn't anything for us to walk into a clothing store and walk out with six thousand dollars worth of new gear. Then we would go to Footlocker or a shoe store like that to buy up a few pairs of shoes a piece. But I hadn't made any big purchases at that point, other than my house. Everybody kept boosting me up to buy a real nice ride, but I wasn't budging.

Earlier that year during Memorial weekend this girl from New Jersey came down with my cousin Patricia. My cousin Jeff was having a big concert at his club, Solid Gold, and everybody was there- all my family, cousins, homeboys; it was a huge concert. Jeff had some of the hottest acts in the music business there all on one night.

I spent most of the night backstage hanging out with Jeff and chilling with all the acts. My cousin Patricia and her friend were back there too. Her name was Stacy. Stacy was light skinned, had a bob cut that was long on one side and shorter on the other. Her hair covered one side of her face, that was the hot style back then thanks to Halle Berry. At any rate, she was one of the baddest chics at the concert, and I had to push up on her. We hit it off early and ended up waking up together in a hotel room the next morning (You get the point). She worked for a big bank in Jersey City. She was a little older and making close to a hundred thousand dollars a year, so I had to stay in contact with her; she was bad.

I would fly her down to the beach for the weekend from time-to-time throughout the year, and we would just enjoy each other until she flew out. She would buy me expensive clothes from Jersey and ship them to my father's house every now and then. She wanted a relationship, but that long-distance thing wasn't going to work for me, especially in my line of work.

But anyhow, I flew her down one weekend and we ended up hanging out at Solid Gold. You gotta remember that Jeff was a multi-millionaire. His expensive taste and flashy persona was at an all-time high around then, and he always tried to get me to go out and buy expensive things. He'd called me a thousand times telling me about exotic cars his friends had for sale-Lamborghinis, Ferraris, big body Benzes and was trying to get me to buy one. I would always laugh it off and tell him that I wasn't going to waste a whole bunch of money on something to drive. Stacy thought the same; that I should go out there get an expensive car. I felt like buying one was like putting a big sign on my forehead that said *'Arrest me, I'm a drug dealer'*. But that night, Jeff let me and her drive his Porsche back to the hotel. The feeling it gave me was all it took. I had to get me something.

I ended up running across a nearly-new Toyota Land Cruiser for sale. Uncle Ty was always going to the auction to buy cars for his lot and ran across a guy who was trying to sell it. The guy ran into some financial problems right after he brought it. It only had four thousand miles on it. It was a Forrest green color, but it had a special paint on it that made it look black at night. I loved it. I loved it enough to spend sixty-thousand dollars cash on it. It had been my dream ride for a while, and now I had it.

CHAPTER 15 – THE POWELL BOYS

In 96' life began coming at me real fast. It wasn't just the money. It was all of the real things in life that shape and mold who we are, that was beginning to matter more and more...

M.Green, the white guy who was buying weed from Uncle Ty, had grown his cocaine business. He was getting to some cash and loved the thrills in life. One of those thrills was driving fast. If you couple that with heavy drinking, you come up with a deadly combination.

He'd just brought a brand new Ford Thunderbird. He didn't have it long at all. One night after he'd been drinking all day, he opened it up on one of the back roads and got into a serious accident. Luckily he didn't get killed, but he did lose his leg.

It was a tragic thing, but the reality is; the dope game doesn't stop for anything. People get locked up, people get murdered, shot, etc-but the game never stops. Right after the incident, his father started coming around. He'd seen what type of money his son was making and didn't want to lose an opportunity to keep it coming. He didn't know much about the dope game, but he knew enough to hustle a little. That's exactly what he did. He would hustle an ounce or two at a time, and soon, he was buying a big 8. At that point, he needed help. Every now and then my dad or Tim would drive packages to him since they were so close by. After a while, Tim was spending more time over there showing him how to work his package. No one saw what would happen a year later coming...

Sally was bringing more work each time, she had to. We had cornered a major portion of the cocaine business in southeastern North Carolina. Our business spanned from Georgetown, S.C to Greenville, North Carolina. The demand was high, and we were doing a great job of distribution.

Rooster, Skeeter Rock and a few more of our crew, Steim and Red, moved to the beach. Now we were moving coke in Hallsboro and had a nice influx of cash bubbling at the beach. It was all beautiful, but the Feds were slowly closing in right under our noses. A few of my family members down on the beach got locked up and people in the area began warning us. The Feds were arresting a few people from the area and they were telling us that they had asked a whole bunch of questions about us. They were asking about the 'Powell Boys' in North and South Carolina. We paid attention and moved more cautious, but think about it...the U.S government is a powerful beast; a beast almost impossible to elude. It was only a matter of time.

One of the most beautiful days of my life happened in the middle of it all. It was the day that my first child was born, Majid. The feeling was indescribable, and if you've brought a child into this world, you understand why. The one thing that sticks out about that day is the constant thought of stopping. I held him in my arms and remember wanting to watch him grow. I wanted to be there in his life every day; as much as I could. I didn't have that growing up; I didn't want to be the father that my dad was. I could easily provide, but providing is just one single part of being a parent-I wanted to be there.

But the reality of it...I couldn't stop. Dealing drugs was my life; the only thing I knew. I'd never had a job of any kind and only a high school diploma. There wasn't a job on the planet that I qualified for that would allow me to maintain my lifestyle. I had to keep going.

I guess after a certain point, every hustler comes up with their number. It's the number that everybody says that once they hit it, they'll quit. I'd hit my number already, three-hundred thousand. Once I hit it, I never had the notion of stopping or even coming up with a new number-I just hustled harder. We all did.

With Majid being born, the few cousins in South Carolina getting locked up, and the Feds asking about us, I knew it was time to really put some money up; just in case anything happened. I purchased a safe and kept it in one of the rooms in my grandparent's house. Over a course of time I kept throwing money in there. Ten grand here, a thousand dollars there, fifteen-thousand here and there; just stacking. My grandparents were extremely modest people. I never trusted anyone with money, but I knew my grandmother wouldn't have touched a dime of it, not even if she really needed it. Before the end of 96', I counted two hundred-seventy eight thousand dollars in there. I put the other twenty-two thousand in there to make it an even three. It was a good feeling to know I'd put away that much money, especially when I still had over a hundred thousand in working capital, a few kilos of cocaine, and people in the street owing me money.

A few months after Majid was born, Tootie popped up pregnant again. It was that same feeling all over again. We were growing our own family, and at the rate I was going, retiring before thirty was a realistic aspiration. I ended up buying another safe to put in my grandparent's. It didn't take long to put a hundred thousand in there.

Raz and Sally still had their differences. When Sally would come through, she would still complain about how slow he was to pay her. He was paying her, but he was always in arrears. Once, when she was hot as fire at him, she spilled the beans.

See the whole time we were thinking that Raz was the mastermind behind his whole operation; that wasn't how it was. Sally had been running cocaine for years for different people. Over that many years she'd seen people get locked up, snaked out of money and everything else. Well, the people she was running cocaine for would always turn her on to other people that were looking for a good runner. Over a course of years she built relationships with big coke connects all up and down the east coast. She was actually the one that turned Raz on to all of his new connects.

Basically, if Sally really wanted to, she could have been one of the biggest coke dealers in the U.S. She had the connects, and on top of that, she knew the foot soldiers that moved the work. We were spending at least a half-million dollars a month with her. On top of that, she knew hustlers in a lot of other places that were spending the same, or close to it. She was loyal. That's a rare quality in the dope game. That's the reason we got a long so well for so many years.

Just like we all thought, my dad shut the club down. We knew it wouldn't take too long. Once his heroin addiction ceased; the El Derado did to. He made a great attempt to make us all believe that he was going to keep it open, build on to the building, and expand the parking lot, but none of that ever happened. It started with him saying he wanted to shut it down for a little while because our names were buzzing too much with the feds. But after he closed for a few weeks, he just never opened back up. That was cool because everybody was too busy.

Uncle Ty was trying his best to talk him into leaving it open. Ty always believed that every hustler needed a legal hustle to account for all the money they were making. To be honest, that's what every hustler should have done, but as hard as we were going, there wasn't really much time to do anything else. His car lot had grown tremendously over the years. At one point he had a little over one hundred cars on his lot. It worked out well for him because he could show that he was making legal money, and he could switch up the car he drove every day.

Tim, Dog, Tootie and I went down to the Bahamas during that time. It was beautiful-gave us a chance to get away and clear our heads...

Everything was going great with me and Tootie, but come on, I still had my issues. I was still flying Stacy in to the beach from time-to-time, and I'd met a few chics in New York that I would fly in from time-to-time. Jeff was spontaneous and knew I would travel with him at the drop of a dime. We would fly out often and go on mini shopping sprees up top. It was cool because we would get clothes that nobody could find around here. We always met women up there and would always end up flying a few of them in and show-ing them the times of their lives at the beach. There was this one chic, Kani, we met in New York at a strip club we went to. She was something like a madam. She would fly down with five or six girls at a time. They had their own money, so when they came the only thing we had to do was get them a condo or two on the water for a few days. Kani just loved hanging out with us down there. When she came, she always brought the party with her. If I had to guess, I probably slept with fifteen of the girls she brought down. The boys ran through them too. My weakness with women was a whole lot worse than my father's. You know the apple doesn't fall far from the tree. There's a whole lot of truth in that cliché.

Tootie would always bring Majid to Hallsboro to see my father and grandparents. I'd been thinking about getting a dog and ran across this white pit bull puppy a fiend wanted to trade for some rock. I took it up the street to my grandparent's to show Tootie. She was in love with it from first site. We ended up naming him Butch. Over the years, Butch became a staple of the barn. It was funny as hell. If a person was coming up there to spend just a little bit of money, he barked at them like he wanted to eat them. If they came to spend big bread, he was quiet as a church mouse. We loved that dog-kept him right behind the barn just in case someone ever tried to sneak back there and try something. He would get his chance the day the feds came...

Close to the end of that year, Dog and Tim kept talking about this girl that was working in Chase. Chase was an urban clothing store in Whiteville that carried the latest Fashions from New York.

It was one of those spots that we would go into and spend thousands of dollars at.

Tim was saying stuff like *"Pete I promise you this got to be the finest chic I seen in-my-life homeboy."* Me and Tim always had similar taste, and if he told you something; it was one-hundred percent true.

"You got to go up there cousin, I'm telling you. I done tried to get her number, and she ain't budging. Hell, we spent bout three thousand up there and she still ain't give me the damn number. Pete, you might be able to get her. She ain't got no man neither." Tim said.

Dog told me how fine she was, but she was too young for him. He told her that he had a nephew for her that he was going to send up there, me. They talked about her so much, I had to go up there and see this chic.

I didn't go right away, but one day while I was riding through Whiteville I decided to stop by Chase. As soon as I walked in, I saw her. The Chinese lady that owned the store always spoke to us when we walked in because we spent so much money there, but this time I couldn't focus on what she was talking about. I made a b-line straight towards this Angel I was looking at.

She was helping two guys, and from the looks of it they were flirting with her, so I just walked around the area of the store she was in and waited. She was only about 5'4. Her hair was long and straightened; skin was absolutely flawless-more of a dark caramel tone. She was athletic, not muscular, but college cheerleader-type build. She was gorgeous, but just observing her, her spirit was what got me.

I could tell that she wasn't feeling those guys at all but she smiled and engaged them the whole while. As soon as she had a split second she told me that she would be with me shortly, as she smiled and looked me dead in my eyes. It was a mesmerizing short moment. She had me gone from the second she acknowledged me. I waited, but did a whole lot of watching in the process.

When she got finished and came over I cut straight to the chase. *"What's your name sweetheart?"*She smiled and kept it professional. *"I'm Marie, and this shirt that you're looking at really goes well with your frame."* She said, as she showed me one of the shirts on one of the clothing racks. I really could have cared less about the shirt.

"My uncle told you about me the other day, I'm Petey." I said, but she just looked like she had no idea who I was talking about.

"I'm Petey Powell...anyway, everybody has been telling me about you, so I decided to stop by and see how good of a saleswoman you are." And I gave her that 'I'm feeling you' look.

Long story short, I walked out of that store with about three grand worth of stuff and this girl didn't even give me her number. Smdh

I gave her my pager number. Usually the women I met hit me the same day or the next day, not Marie. It was three or four days before I heard anything from her. Then when she paged me, I was so busy at the barn I couldn't call back right away. It took me about an hour or two before I called her. Then, I was so busy, I had to catch myself being too rushed on the phone. The next day I called and we planned to go to the beach that coming weekend. Wasn't really a whole bunch of convo, I was busy as hell that week.

I got Jeff to book a condo for the weekend, and that Friday afternoon, I picked her up and we rolled out. She had no idea that I was a drug dealer and that was the thing that got my attention. She hadn't heard of me before so we got to know each other for real. The Land Cruiser was a surprise to her; she didn't know what I was driving when I came to Chase. She was bright, put two and two together and figured out that whatever I was doing wasn't exactly the most legal of businesses.

That weekend, I showed her some things she'd never experienced. We started out at one of the finest restaurants on the beach. I don't remember which one to be honest; I frequented them all. Then we went to the condo. It was nice, but really not the nicest I'd ever booked. At any rate, her mind was blown. That night, we hooked up with Jeff and went to Solid Gold. That's what did it. Everybody who was anybody came and spoke to me in VIP. She fit right in. I was in awe of her poise throughout the night.

We didn't sleep together, nor did we even sleep in the same bed that night. I courted her for a few months. It took a while for me to grow on her to just be frank, but after we got to that point, I had her heart. Tootie was still my queen, but Marie slowly grabbed a piece of my heart. We fell in love. It was a slow process, but it was organic and beautiful.

At this point in my life, I'd become more ambitious than I'd ever been. With the feds being curious, a baby and another baby on the way; I knew it was time to get legal. I sought out business opportunities time and time again, but none of what I was seeing was going to work for me. The perfect opportunity came by chance, by way of a guy who borrowed some money from me named Drew.

Drew owed me a lump sum and was facing some time for trafficking. He owned a clothing store in Whiteville, right on the main street that ran through downtown. When he felt like it was inevitable that he was going to have to do time, he offered a sweet deal to me. He was going to give me his store and his entire inventory. The only thing I would have to do was pay the rent on the storefront. Uncle Ty always got on us about cleaning up our money; what better way, and it fit me.

I changed the name of the business to Street Fashions and De-
signs. I sold urban clothes, mixtapes, oils, and clothing accessories
out of there. I let my mom and Tracy run the business. After a
short time in business, it became profitable. In fact, it did so well
that I decided to open another urban clothing store close to me and
Tootie's home in Shallotte, Fashion Zone. Tootie ran the store. It
was the only place you could get urban clothing in the area. She ran
a television vision commercial and got radio promotion spots for a
short period of time. It didn't take long for that business to become
profitable as well.

Here I was. I had a nice home, two businesses, two girlfriends,
a child, and another child on the way. On top of all of that, I was
one of the biggest drug dealers in the state. For many, that would
have been what they considered success. My ambition wouldn't allow me to think that way. I wanted more.

We still partied like we were getting paid to. This one Thursday
night we all loaded up to go to Wilmington for a big concert. Foxy
Brown was doing a show at the Palomino night club. She was one
of the hottest female rappers in music at the time. It was me, my
homeboy Chic, Dog, and Kendal. We were right up front at the concert with everybody in Wilmington who was anybody. She was so
fine; all I could do was stare at her. That was one fine chocolate
woman.

That night when the concert was over, one of the people in her entourage screamed out ***"After Party at the Hilton!!!"*** over the mic when everybody was leaving out. It was cool with us. We had already checked into our room at the Hilton, right on the waterfront.

When we pulled up to the hotel, there were hundreds of people waiting in a long line at the front entrance. There were also a whole lot of police. We walked right pass them all and this cop tried to stop us and ask us where we were going. I just showed him my key and told him we were going up to our room. There was a whole bunch of people in line that knew us, so people thought we were part of Foxy's entourage. We laughed about it the whole way up to the room.

When we got to our floor and were walking down the hallway, Foxy was walking down the hallway with a few of her girls. All of them were fine and we all kind of stared at each other in passing. I wasn't going to miss the opportunity to speak. I told her she did a great job that night and smiled. One of my best commodities has always been my teeth, and when she saw me smile she gave me a compliment on them. Come to find out, they were staying in the room right next to us.

We called downstairs and got the front desk to connect the call to their room. It surprised me when she was the one that picked up the phone. I told her that I was the guy who'd just passed her down the hallway. She stopped me right there *"**with the pretty teeth...**"* I immediately invited her and her girls over to party with us for the night. A few minutes later, there was a knock at the door. It was her and some other girls that were with her.

It's a small world, Chic and one of them had actually met before at a party down on the beach. Foxy was looking like a bag of money, absolutely gorgeous. She told me that she'd noticed me at the concert. I thought she was just talking, until she described what I had on. By that time, I'd already taken off the sweater I was wearing and she described it to a tee. When I pulled it out, she giggled and said *"**I told you I noticed you.**"*

She sat down on my lap and we talked for a while, while my homies and her girls all chatted across the room. Everything was going good, until a knock came on the door. When I opened it, it was her brother. He asked if she was in there and then he called her outside. We all heard them arguing through the door.

*"**What you doing?!?! You don't even know these dudes and you all in they room hanging out like you from here!!! As soon as I walk in, they got a gun and all that money on the counter! You out here wilding for real! Yall need to come on back to the room...**"* He said. She argued back, basically telling him that she was grown and her money was the only reason he was eating anyway.

When she came back into the room she apologized for him and said they had to go. She invited us all up to another concert she was doing that next night in Raleigh, and gave me the hotel number she was going to be at. She wanted me to come up and we were going to hang out after the concert and the next day.

I had to take Tootie and Majid to a doctor's appointment the next day, so I told her I couldn't make it but I would try. I ended up not going but she didn't forget me. I would find that out a few years later at the airport in Atlanta...

The birth of my second child, Malik, fueled me to go even harder. This time, when Tootie gave birth, the feeling of not wanting to hustle didn't come. I knew hustling was short lived, and don't get it twisted, I didn't want to do it forever, but I knew I needed to capitalize at this moment in my life.

Dent wasn't around much then. He'd always been a white-collar type of criminal and when he wasn't coming around that's exactly what he was doing; white-collar crimes. He got jammed up, not exactly sure what for, but he was sentenced to a few years in prison. That's where he would eventually take his last breath.

Sally was working overtime at this phase of my life. Sometimes she would come down and stay at Dog's house. That became a safer place for her to come to because of all the traffic we were getting at the barn-she didn't need to be around that. Quite often, when she made her drop, we would have twenty or thirty kilos of cocaine lying on the bar in Dog's kitchen. It was always a sight to see, but it was just a normal part of the life we lived. At any given time, I could put my hands on ten kilos of my own, and at least four hundred thousand dollars. With my assets included, I was a millionaire. I'm not quite sure, but if I had to guess, as a collective we were worth well over five million dollars.

Uncle Ulysses was cool at the barn, but every man wants his own space and own life. One of the fiends that came by had an opportunity for him to go out to Tennessee working a light weight construction gig that was paying well. He was an elderly man by then, but he could handle the workload. We hated to see him go because he was so cool to have around. We never knew that would be the last time we saw him. A few months after he got out there, he died of natural causes. You never know when God is going to call your number.

Shortly after Uncle Ulysses died, Cajun started coming around. Cajun was from New Orleans. He'd been serving time in North Carolina and happened to become pen pals with one of the ladies in the neighborhood. He came straight from prison to Hallsboro and started working for Moe doing construction. The lady he'd hooked up with didn't have any idea that Cajun was smoking crack, and it didn't take long for him to find us. With Hallsboro being so small, gossip travels around the neighborhood at the speed of light.

She kicked him out as soon as she found out he was smoking. Cajun had been around a little while and spent a whole lot of time and money at the barn. Pop loved him. Cajun turned out to be a good dude after we got to know him a little.

Pop let Cajun stay at the barn for two hundred dollars a month after he got kicked out. It worked out better than expected. See, Cajun was like Rob Base. He was a fiend, but you could leave him dope to sell. We started him out real small, maybe a half ounce or an ounce. Then, it got to the point that we could trust him with big 8's, then kilos. To be a fiend, Cajun was a better hustler than most of the hustlers I knew at that time. With him at the barn, that gave us a lot more freedom to leave. We didn't miss a dollar. It was a crack addicts dream. He had all the dope he wanted to smoke, a roof over his head, and even made a hell of a lot of money.

Tim was still going over there to M. Green's helping his dad work his package. Well, earlier in that year, a fiend who knew a whole bunch of drug dealers from South Carolina kept telling Big Mike about this connect that she knew that was selling kilos for dirt cheap. My father loved meeting new connects. Buying as much cocaine as we were buying, it was always a good practice to have a few different connects to go to. You never knew who was going to have the cheapest price and best quality of coke.

Just so happens, the connect that she was referring to was a white lady named Lisa. Lisa wasn't bad looking at all. We didn't know that Big Mike had bought a key from her until the second time she came around. Me and Tim walked into the house one day and there she was sitting in the living room with my dad. He called us to the kitchen and told us that he'd just bought a kilo from her, then he showed us the work. It was strange from Jump Street. She sold it to him in thirty-six individual ounces, all in individual Crown Royal bags. Nobody did that type of thing. We looked at my father like he was crazy, and explained to him that he didn't know whether or not she was the police or the feds, but he'd been hustling so long; he didn't care that we didn't approve of it.

She came a few times after then and on one occasion, her and M. Green's dad met. He was in love with her from first sight. They ended up exchanging numbers and doing business together. We didn't know that they'd hooked up at first and then he spilled the beans to us.

A time came that Big Mike was out of town, I wasn't around, Dog wasn't around, and maybe Uncle Ty was busy-that M. Green's dad needed to re-up. Tim was at his house and told him to wait. I'd just stashed a few kilos in a new spot and hadn't told Tim where it was at yet. I was handling some business with Jeff at the beach and would dared not tell him where it was at over the phone.

That was Green's dad's perfect excuse to go see Lisa. They asked me if I wanted to meet them somewhere close to where they were going and ride with them there, I declined. When they got there to link up with her, the feds closed in on them. Lisa had been working with them the whole while. Tim ended up having to serve two years in the fed joint behind what happened. The feds didn't drop down on my dad for buying the work from her just yet. They were still building their case.

And just when I thought things couldn't go anymore south, Marie popped up pregnant...

I was financially able and knew Marie would be a great mother from the beginning. The only thing I had to do was to hide it from Tootie. When you have enough money, you can hide anything on this planet. Money and cocaine was one thing I had plenty of.

CHAPTER 16 – LIKE FATHER LIKE SON

With two kids already, a third one on the way, and the feds clos-ing in fast, the push to get out of the game was heavy. Jeff always had something up his sleeve, and every time he could let me get in on one of his hustles, he would. He'd planned a ton of concerts for that year and the following year. He was booking artist at the Gold Club and other clubs at the beach, at different spots around N.C and S.C, and even in Atlanta.

I would give him sixty to eighty grand investment per show and we always made a ton of money. Jeff's hustles were almost always full proof. We booked artist like Red Man, Method Man, Cash Money, Jagged Edge-whoever was hot, we had them booked to do a concert. We put on a show at the Palomino in Wilmington and the Red Roper in Fayetteville the next day featuring Jr. Mafia. To give you an idea of how big the shows were that we were putting on, the show at the Palomino was the first performance they did after Big-gie Smalls died.

All the shows were epic, and most of the time we showed the artist who performed a better time than they'd ever had on a booking. When we picked them up from the airport, we would have the nicest limos money could buy transporting them. We put them up in the nicest hotels or condos some of them had ever stayed in at that point in their career. Sometimes they were supposed to be in town for two days and ended up staying the whole week because we showed them such a good time. All of the acts were amazed at the treatment we gave them. They couldn't believe a bunch of country dope boys were making so much money. It was what it was. We were self-made multi-millionaires in rural America.

Dog ended up getting married to the baby mama of two of his kids during that time. He had a small ceremony and a whole bunch of people didn't know. Finally, Uncle Dog handed in his player card. It kinda made me want to do the same-kinda.

As soon as Marie had the baby, my first daughter Maisha, her mom and I had a deep conversation at her house. She wanted to really know that I was going to be there for my child. I let her know that I was always going to take care of my responsibilities, especially my kids. We thought it would be best if she stayed with Dog and his wife. They had a place in Whiteville at the time and had extra space. Dog felt like Marie would be good company for his wife, and his wife could help out with the baby.

Everything worked out great but somehow, Tootie caught wind that I had a baby with a girl in Whiteville. She didn't have any concrete evidence, so I lied and lied and kept lying about it. She wasn't too hard on me about it at first; she was just suspicious as hell. As time went by, it worried the crap out her. It was killing her, but I kept dispelling it as a rumor.

Tootie would go to the beauty salon in Whiteville. You know what goes on in those things; a whole bunch of gossiping. Those girls kept telling her that I had another baby. By this time she'd found it in her heart to stay by my side and believe me. She basically kept telling them to stay out of our business.

Then, like always, it happened...

Jeff and I had just returned home from New York. I had to take my truck to Whiteville to get some new tires on it so Jeff picked me up from the tire shop and we went to Hallsboro. By this time, Mont had dropped out of school and was selling drugs, just like the rest of us. Yeah...the once bright highly-intelligent little guy got out there in the street. Jeff and I went to a trailer that he was trapping out of to chill out for a second. Dog was over there at the time.

We weren't there long at all, maybe an hour or two, and I heard Dog scream out *"Oh Shi#!!!!"* I was in the backroom at the time, and peeped down the hallway to see what was going on. Dog came down the hallway to get me and tell me what was happening...

"Man, stay back here. Tootie outside..."

I really didn't think much of it when he said it, so I looked at him like *'why you tripping like that for'?* But then he told me the rest...

"Bruh, she got Marie and the baby in the car!"

My heart stopped. Somehow Tootie found out where Marie was staying and went by there to see if the rumors were true. I was caught red handed and couldn't believe this woman had picked up Marie and the baby. Then the door opened and Tootie walked inside.

The first person she spoke to was Jeff. *"Jeff, the favorite cousin...Why you ain't tell me that ya boy had a baby and a wife staying over there in Whiteville?"* She was playing it calm and seemed to be in good spirits. She was being sarcastic as hell.

"And Dog, you the good Samaritan Uncle huh? Got her staying in yo house like everything ok. Smiling in my face every time you see me. Ummm Hmmm..."

By that time I was walking down the hallway ready to face the music.

"Oh Petey-Powell! Baby, why you ain't tell me bout this beautiful baby you done went out there and had?" I couldn't do nothing but look at her while she stood there with that sarcastic smile on her face.

"I don't know how ya'll had this beautiful baby, but ya'll did. Yes ya'll did." She said. *"Well, I'll have your stuff packed up for you when you get home. Damn ya'll done had a beautiful baby. Im goin' take them back home and Petey I should be done packing your stuff in the next few hours..."*

I found out that she had went to Marie and told her who she was, asking whether or not it was true. Marie denied everything over and over when she came, then Tootie told her that I was denying the baby. That was the nail in the coffin. When Tootie said that, Marie spilled the beans. Then they all packed up in Tootie's car and came over.

That night, I went back home in Shallotte. She didn't pack my things up like she said, and we even tried to sort things through. She made me promise that I wouldn't deal with Marie anymore and that I wouldn't cheat on her ever again. That didn't happen, and it sent her into a whirlpool of stress.

Tootie needed some serious R & R. I'd put her through hell. So me, Dog, Jeff and Tootie decided to go on a small vacation to Jamaica. A week before we flew into Jamaica, Me and Dog left Cajun a few kilos and decided to go down to the Freaknik in Atlanta. Tootie begged me not to go, but I'd already made plans with all my homeboys. She didn't even know I was in Atlanta the first day or so. When I called her and told her, she flipped out.

"I knew yo ass was going to go down there!" she said. I ended up telling her that I was going to meet her at the airport in Atlanta. I got her to bring some more money because I went to the strip club in Atlanta and spent a few thousand. She also packed some clothes of mine and bought them to me. Jeff was always last minute so he flew straight to Jamaica and met us at the hotel.

We cut the fool in Atlanta. I had all my homeboys down there and I promise you we went to every party, every strip club, and event that Freaknik had to offer. Me and Dog got Chic to drop us off at the airport when it was time to head out. Tootie was already there waiting. She'd flown in from the beach and was connecting in Atlanta.

On our way through the airport the strangest thing happened. We saw all of these people taking pictures of someone. We knew it had to be a celebrity or someone important, but we couldn't see exactly who it was.

As we got closer, we realized that it was Foxy Brown and Kurupt. They'd gotten engaged right before then and were in the airport catching a flight leaving Atlanta. Chic went over to speak with her, and took a picture. When she looked over and saw me, I knew that she remembered me because of the way she looked over at me. She ended up telling Chic to tell me that she said hello. We met eyes and smiled at each other as she, Kurupt, and the crowd that followed passed by. Very small world.

Dog, Tootie, and I took off for Jamaica and met Jeff at the hotel. His flight came in a few hours after ours so by the time he got there; we were already having a ball. Tootie and I spent most of the trip with each other, but I had the chance to hang out with Dog and Jeff. One of those nights we got missing all night long. Tootie was mad as hell the next morning when we got back, and had every right.

What happened was that one of Jeff's associates had flown in and was doing some business there. We hooked up with him and went out partying that night. In the middle of all that partying we did, the guy had a meeting with someone at the club we were at about some cocaine, damn near one hundred kilos. The guy who he was dealing with had some of the sexiest females I'd ever seen in my life with him at the club. He set each of us up with one of them and we spent the night with those girls. It was well worth Tootie cursing me out the next morning. At least that's what I thought.

The trip ended up being a nice break, but it wasn't enough to stop what was inevitable. The cheating got to be too much for her to bear. She was still hearing rumors about Marie and I, and she didn't have to question them one bit; they were very true. I ended up leaving and buying a house on the outskirts of Whiteville-away from everybody. When Marie gave me the news that she was pregnant again, shortly after I moved in, I moved her in.

I didn't completely leave Tootie alone, we had two children, but we kept our distance for the most part. She was the second love of my life, I'd put her through the ringer, and she needed her space to get herself back together. I was toxic to her and I understood.

I was in the barn sitting down on the couch downstairs just thinking about everything early one morning. What I'd done to Dawana, Tootie, dropping out of college, selling cocaine...all of it was on my mind. My dad came in and caught me there. He didn't say anything at first; he just sat down on the other end of the couch. Out of nowhere, without even looking in my direction, he asked me a question that I'd never expect for him to ask.

"Pete, why did my wife leave me?"

He was looking straight forward when he asked, staring at the wall. I didn't really know what to say when those words came out of his mouth, and had no clue why he was asking.

"Pop, you were never there. You've been doing the same thing since I was a kid, and other than the money, you've never been there. She got tired man. You can't expect a woman worth having to keep putting up with all of this. You were her everything. She still loves you; you just gotta get it together. I gotta get my stuff together, because I'm just like you..."

He didn't respond. In the moment I glanced at him to see what kind of emotion he had on his face, I realized that I was just like the man sitting at the other end of that couch. I looked like him, I loved women like him, I hustled like him, and I was wasting my precious days on this earth away just like him. I told him about the baby on the way, and he said congratulations, but he didn't have any advice to give me. We just sat there for a few before Cajun came downstairs. As soon as Cajun came down and started talking to Big Mike, that was my queue to leave.

I'd watched my father change over the past few years. He loved the way he loved. He may not have been affectionate as other folks, and he may not have been as verbal as other folks, but he loved. The man did something in front of my eyes that millions of people think is impossible, he beat his heroin addiction. I saw moments that he just wanted to stop selling cocaine, but the world around him wanted him to be Big Mike. I'll never try to absolve any of the wrong any of us did, but I did see the heart of my dad-the side of him that mattered the most to me at the end of the day. The same with Dog, me, and Uncle Ty; good people-caught up doing the wrong things...

CHAPTER 17 – THE EMPIRE CRUMBLES

In early 99', the empire that we worked so hard to build came to an end in the blink of an eye...

Dent was just about to get out of prison. I know he was probably feeling on top of the world. A few weeks before his release, the warden called him into his office and informed him that he had a federal indictment on a drug case; ours. Dent had a heart attack right there. He dropped dead right there in the warden's office.

He was the first to be informed of our case...

For the rest of us, it started with the DMV trying to get in contact with Uncle Ty. They'd been trying their best to reach him for a few days, even went through the length of calling my grandmother. They claimed that there were some issues with some of the paperwork for some of the vehicles on his lot. Unc' didn't think anything of it. They were always bothering him about paperwork or something. The day that he was supposed to go to DMV to handle it, I'd planned to meet him at the gym in Whiteville. The plan was for him to go to DMV and then come to the gym right after he went. I went to the gym, and waited, and waited, and waited. Unc' never showed.

What happened was-he did make it to DMV. As soon as he got there, he was picked up for a parole violation while he was in there and taken to the county jail. It was BS, and when he was in the county that day, he figured out that they were actually picking him up to face the federal indictment.

When I returned to the barn, after waiting all that time for him at the gym, it was busy as I don't know what. The first person I served as soon as I pulled up wanted a quarter kilo. Cajun had run out of coke earlier that morning, so I had a group of people waiting on me just as soon as I got there. The traffic was absolutely crazy from that point. It was an exceptionally busy day.

Well, I noticed that this car pulled up into the driveway that looked like an undercover sheriff's car, and then a man that got out of it that definitely looked like some type of officer of the law. There were a few other people that were walking up the driveway just before he arrived, so they got a good look. Cajun and I cleaned up shop. He took the last bit of work that was in there and took off out the back door of the barn across the field. Thank God there wasn't much left in there at that particular time.

When the couple of people that were walking up came through the door of the barn, I was standing by the back door ready to take off just in case there was a raid or something. They told me the news that changed my life when they got in there...It was a federal agent.

I did what any person in their right mind would; I ran like hell. I went straight out the back door of the barn through the field to a neighbor's house that was a little ways away. I could see the barn from her porch, but I was far enough away that it was impossible to make out who I was from there.

She was inside. I startled her a bit when I ran onto her porch like that, but when she saw it was me, she quickly opened the door and told me to hurry inside. I didn't know where Cajun had ran to, but from the looks of it, a few more undercover cars had pulled into the driveway and they had taken my father outside. I could hear Butch behind the barn barking like crazy, and then all of a sudden I heard a man screaming at the top of his lungs in pain. One of the federal agents had walked behind the barn and gotten bit.

When I got inside her house, it seemed like she was panting harder than I was. ***"Petey, somebody just called and said that a whole bunch of police cars and undercover cars up the road!!!"*** she said. They'd parked up the road from the house and were waiting. For some reason, they had us made out to be extremely violent criminals. As fast as I got into her house and took another look at what was going on through her window, my dad's whole yard was filled with federal agents and sheriff deputies.

The day had come. The day that every hustler has nightmares about and plays over and over through his mind. Everyone knows the rules; it isn't like nobody thinks they're invincible. Hustlers prepare themselves for this day. They stack bail money, have lawyers and bails bondsmen on standby, and if you're lucky enough, you put money to the side just in case you gotta get missing. Whatever the case, you can't elude the inevitable. There's no such thing as 'happily ever after in this game.'

I'd played this day over and over in my head. My first priority was to salvage as much money as I could. The clock started, no time to fumble; run...

Cajun was actually across the field and had seen me when I stepped on my neighbor's porch. He'd made it to the main road and walked there. We were able to borrow my neighbor's car and go to my grandparent's. Soon as I got there, it was straight to the safe. Someone had already called my grandmother's house and told her what was happening. The feds wanted all of us...

I grabbed the four-hundred grand, and talked to my grandma while pacing the floor and peeping out the window to see what was happening. Red Bug was filled with feds, sheriff's, and people riding by to buy dope that hadn't seen what was going on yet, and others that were just being nosey. The news had traveled fast.

Two undercover cars slowly pulled in front of my grandparent's home. I hugged and kissed her, and almost started to run out the back door, but luckily, they didn't pull into the driveway. I knew I couldn't stay there long. I had to make a way across the street to one of the bootleggers. A lot of people were always there. I knew I could get a ride. When I looked at my grandmother's face, I knew. She was the most beautiful spirit I'd ever encountered in my entire life. All of the things she'd ever said to me were all wrapped up in this one moment. The tears came for both of us. That was the last time I saw her...

Tick tock...

I ran out the front door and frantically made my way across the street to the bootlegger's I was trying to get to. Forgive me, but some things are best left unsaid. The bootlegger allowed me to call a true friend of mine to pick me up, and get me up out of Hallsboro. Jeff and I had a concert at the beach that night. We booked Cash Money, and a lot of people were planning to go. There was a lot of people who were going that owed me money that were going to pay me that night. I didn't have a choice; I had to go get my money. My friend came to pick me up and we headed straight to the beach.

They'd picked up Uncle Ty, my dad, and Dog at this point. When I got to the beach, I got my friend to check me into a hotel for the week and we left to go to the show. When I saw Jeff, he was blown away by what was happening. He was also just as scared as I was. We were all connected. In some shape, form, or fashion we'd all broke bread together.

The people that were supposed to bring my money did. That was almost another eighty-thousand. I couldn't find a way to relax while I was there, anybody could have been a federal agent. I actually felt like everybody in that building was. I ended up going to my hotel room and sitting still. I didn't want any phone calls, no pages, I'd thrown my cell phone away in Hallsboro-I just wanted to be with me. Jeff came through the next day to let me know what he found out about what was happening and gave me my portion of the profits from the concert, twenty-eight thousand. He didn't stay long. It wasn't safe for either one of us for him to stay long.

Now that I'd gotten my hands on some salvageable cash, it was time to get my hands on some of my work. I didn't know how many stash spots they hit, nor was I thinking about what I knew they were going to take. I wasn't taking any chances. There was one spot that I knew they would have never gone if they ever came. It was an older friend of the family's house. Right in her back yard, in the trunk of one of the three older cars she had sitting back there rusting, was five kilos of cocaine.

If I could find someone to handle those five kilos, I would always have cash. It takes money to run. You can't have a job; you can't be out in the street hustling. You're facing the U.S government. They have all the resources in the world to catch you, it's just a matter of when you get tired of running, or when you run out of money. I needed to find someone. The man I chose was Juice. He knew the game, was loyal, my connects knew him, and the people I dealt with. He was perfect.

When I called him, he already knew what I needed him to do, he just didn't know where my work was at; nobody knew. On his way to get the work, there was a road block set up on Old Lumberton road. Everyone thought they'd set the road block up to check cars for me. None of us would have ever guessed that they had an indictment on Juice. When he was going through the road block, they got him.

The next person in line was Rooster. He was almost just as perfect as Juice. Juice had just been around me a lot more often than Rooster. He went and successfully picked up the five kilos. As soon as he did, I got the hell away from the beach. I headed for Raleigh.

I could have went anywhere in the U.S I wanted to go, but I wanted to stick around until I knew exactly what was happening with everyone. I floated from Raleigh to Durham for the next two months. I was going from hotel to hotel.

The women in my life saw me often. Tootie would come frequently, so did Marie, and a few other girls. The feds had been harassing them, telling them that they knew where I was, and how bad of a person I was-just being assholes. Tootie, as expected, would go off on them. Marie was pregnant and they still harassed the hell out of her.

I called Dawana. She'd heard about what happened, everybody did, and she cried like I'd never heard her cry before on that phone. She came to see me. For the first time in our lives, we had a real conversation about what I'd been doing all those years. She had every right to think that I was the worst person that ever walked this earth for lying to her for all those years, but she didn't. She looked at me like she'd always looked at me. She was heartbroken, but even more so than the heart break, she was afraid for me.

I would go to clubs-everything that I normally did, but I didn't do anything flashy. For the first time in a long time, I didn't want to stand out. I'd lived all those years standing out, having all those eyes on me, a whole bunch of people wanted to walk in my shoes... No one wanted to be in my shoes now.

I saw people that I'd been good to for years, now, I saw them for who they truly were. Some only cared about me because of my money, others actually gave a damn. Didn't take long at all to figure out who was who.

The feds harassed my grandparents, my mom, my family members and friends the whole time I ran. My mom and Tracy moved back into the house right after it happened. The feds would be parked behind the barn, sitting in the woods behind the house and following them everywhere they went, thinking that would lead them to me. All of their phones where tapped. When I made calls to them from payphones, it would be on my way out of whatever city I was in. Raleigh was the central hub of my run for a while. Rooster was flipping my package and giving money to Marie. He was also bringing money up to me from time-to-time. I would go to Fayetteville and stay a while, Greensboro, Greenville; wherever the wind blew me. Every gas station, newspaper and the news in the area had my picture in it with a cash reward for any information on my whereabouts. They made it very clear that I was armed and dangerous. That was a lie. Most people who actually knew me would take the wanted posters down whenever they saw them.

Rumor has it that I would come back to Hallsboro while I was on the run from time-to-time wearing a dress and a big wig. It's a big rumor that's been going on since a little while after I started running. People would tell folks that I would walk through Hallsboro, still selling dope; in a damn dress. Now you gotta be honest. That's a helluva clever idea, but that never happened. I don't know where people came up with that mess from.

Uncle Ty, Dog and my dad decided to take their case to trial. The odds of beating the U.S government are slim to none. Only three percent of the cases that are taken to trial are won. With that being said, their first trial was a mistrial. It blew my mind when I heard. That bought a small ray of hope that they would walk. If that would have happened, I would have turned myself in immediately.

Marie gave birth to my youngest daughter while I ran, Mia. She was born at a hospital on the beach. The second I heard, I went straight to the hospital to see my baby. I didn't care about getting caught, my child was far more important to me. She was as beautiful as all my children and made me realize that my life wasn't over. I just had a dilemma in my life at that point. I didn't know what was going to happen, but I was going to make the best out of whatever came my way.

The second trial sealed my family's fate. The judge gave Dog twenty-seven years. Uncle Ty was given seventeen years. My dad's sentence was harsher than any sentence I'd heard of in my life. The judge gave Big Mike a life sentence, plus twenty years... Imagine hearing that your father was given over a million years in prison.

It was time for me to get away from North Carolina. The feds were still harassing everyone, and to make matters worse, they were harassing Marie with my newborn baby. Her family lived in Philadelphia and we'd talked about her moving up there a lot. They loved me genuinely, so we moved there.

We were able to find a steal on a nice home right in the city. That took a large portion of my money, but it's exactly what I needed to raise my two girls. I would travel from Philadelphia to New

Jersey. I knew that I had to keep moving. Marie and the girls were situated, I felt like the more I stayed away from home, the less chance they had of locating me.

Some of those times I would be in New Jersey, I would fly Dawana in. She was scared as hell by this point. The feds had been questioning her about me. They were coming to her home and her job. They put a lot of pressure on her, and even though she'd never been exposed to this kind of life, she didn't break.

All the girls that I'd flown to the beach from New Jersey and New York would come to see me while I was up in Jersey. A lot of my family and friends who were in the area would come by and see me as well. A lot them genuinely cared and helped me any way they could.

It was hard to see people in D.C. Most of the people I spoke with told me to stay the hell away from D.C. Hell, that's where the J. Edgar Hoover building is. I hung out with a few of my family and friends, but D.C was only short stays.

Every couple weeks, I would still go to Raleigh. I needed to see my boys and Tootie. I never drove. Something as simple as an officer pulling me for a seatbelt ticket would have been disastrous. I wouldn't have any other choice but to run, and ultimately, probably would have gotten caught moments later.

The biggest scare that I had on the run was in Durham. I rode the bus from Philadelphia and almost as soon as I got off, two police officers walked up to me and asked me to step to the side and talk with them for a second.

I stayed calm. They were just police, but they were asking me a ton of questions. They asked me where I was coming from, and I just pointed their attention to the sign at the front of the bus that said Philadelphia in big white letters. I guess they thought I was trying to be an asshole, because they got a whole lot more intense after then.

They asked me my name; I gave them my middle and last name. They wanted to see my I.D, but I didn't have one on me. They gave me this long lecture about how important it is to have identification and that they could arrest me for not having it. They were just harassing for no reason. They opened my bag and saw that I had four thousand cash on me. They gave me hell about why I was traveling with that much money. I told them that I was working construction and that I was coming home for a few days to be with my family.

By that time, Tootie pulled up to pick me up. She could see everything that was happening from across the street in the parking lot. She didn't panic, at least she didn't appear to. When they finished with me, I hopped in that truck and got away as fast as I possibly could. I just knew for sure that they had me. When I returned to Philly, I decided that I needed to be still for a minute. I was tired of running...

CHAPTER 18 – MY HAPPILY EVER AFTER

Marie has always been a thinker. It didn't make much sense for us to have a nice home, have my daughters in an expensive daycare program, and have no legitimate income coming into the home. Looking through the paper, she found a job as a clerk at a Rite-Aid that was only a few blocks away. Her polished-bubbly personality had always made a way for her, this time was no different. After she was hired, she quickly got promoted to assistant manager.

I would take the girls to school in the mornings and stay inside the house most days. Philly became my refuge. I was reclusive, but every once and a while I would get out of the house for fresh air. Seeing different people of all ethnicities walking around with their families would always make me self-actualize. I started out as a small boy in a small rural town, now; I was a fugitive-literally buying time. Each day seemed like it cost more than the previous. Each minute of my freedom became more precious than the last.

When that inevitable day came for me, Marie had just left for work and I'd just dropped my daughters off to daycare. As I came down our street, just before I reached our home, I passed by a younger white guy driving a white mid-sized sedan. It didn't look like any type of car that an undercover would drive, and it was a descent neighborhood, so it wasn't strange to see different people riding through all the time, but something about this car was different. We both took a quick glance at each other as we passed. I took the paranoid feeling I had at that particular moment, as just being paranoid. I was always on edge.

As I walked into our home, I paused for a sec before I stepped inside. Nothing seemed any different than any other day. My routine didn't change. I would drop my daughters off, take a shower, and try my best to relax each day. Sometimes, Marie's brother or her father would stop by for a second, but other than that, that was it. Right as I got out of the shower and was putting on my clothes, there was a loud knock at the door. That wasn't anything different either. Marie's dad would bang on our door almost each time he came. Sometimes we would have the television or radio playing loud and couldn't hear if someone was knocking.

When I almost made it to the door to open it, it burst open just like the door did when the Narcs raided us at Dog's house. Before I had a chance to run or do anything, there were multiple US Marshals coming in with guns drawn, forcing me to the floor. I didn't fight, I didn't say a word. So many things went through my head in those few seconds. The thoughts that stuck out the most were of Majid, Malik, Miasha, and Mia. When they walked me outside to take me in, there were over thirty cars with flashing lights on top of them. The scene was blinding. You would have thought they thought Osama Bin Laden was inside with the number of officers and agents they sent to get me.

I was held in Philadelphia for about two months before they transported me to Raleigh. They'd built a strong case against me, and I was set to face trial in Wilmington. In my short stay in Raleigh, a piece of my heart was ripped out of my chest-my grandmother died.

They didn't let me go to the funeral, nor did they allow my father or Uncle Ty. She was the last person to ever see me cry. That was a tough lost for all of us. They figured we would run if we went to the funeral. We weren't the viscous men that they made us out to be, and that stigma that they put on us wouldn't allow my dad and my Uncle to see the woman who gave birth to them, and loved them every single day of their lives, be put to rest. None of us ever got angry about it; sorrow is a much stronger emotion.

After being transported to Wilmington, the games began. The prosecutor began by telling me that I could walk out that very day. The only thing that I had to do was testify on my cousin Jeff. They wanted Jeff so bad it was sickening.

We all did wrong. Not one person did any more wrong than the next. Maybe Jeff sold more drugs and affected more lives, but look at all the lives my evils affected. We all played a role in the drug trade, there was no doubt about that, but my freedom wasn't worth it. By telling me that I could walk if I testified on Jeff; that would mean that all the lives I ruined meant nothing to them. I told them to give me my sentence and allow me to start repaying my debt to society. I was ready to face the music, and this was a dance that I had to dance alone.

I received a letter from my dad just before I went to trial. Other than sitting on the couch that day in the barn, it was the most intimate thing my father ever shared with me...

"Dear Pete,

I'm sorry that we are communicating under these circumstances. I may have never told you that I love you since you've been an adult, but I want you to know that I love you dearly. We will speak further soon, but I need you to listen close.

They already have it figured out. Son, they want to give you a lot of time. Take it from me. Take the plea deal that they give you. If you take your case to trial, they are going to try to bury you in prison like they did me. Son, I'm already gone for a lifetime, don't end up the same way that I am.

You're young. After you do your time, get out and show my grandbabies a life that I never showed you. Please son. Take the plea. Don't fight them, just take it. Love, Big Mike"

I was sentenced to fifteen years and nine months. I had one request when my sentencing came down. That was to be sent to Butner LSC. That's where Ty and Juice were serving time at during that time. The judge granted my request. Seven months after I was there, Dog was sent there as well; the four of us in the same unit-together again. When we got news that Dre' died in a car accident, it really hurt. The fact that we all had so much time meant that people close to our hearts may not ever see us again. That's one of the harsh consequences of prison that people rarely talk about.

Eventually they picked up Raz, Sally, Jeff, Rooster, and some more of my family in South Carolina. They'd wiped out our whole operation in a matter of months.

It was impossible to be around my father. The facilities that he was serving in were for a higher class of criminal. The first few years were ok, I had some of my close circle with me, and then Uncle Ty was sent to Manchester, Kentucky. It didn't take too long, I was sent there shortly after. My grandfather died while we were there. I was broken; Uncle Ty took it even harder. It was tough watching him go through that. I offered as much comfort as I could, but it hurt him far more than words can describe.

An amazing thing happened after the first few years. The sentencing commission changed the harsh crack laws. My sentence was reduced significantly and so was everyone else's. I was happiest for Big Mike. The life sentence plus twenty years was reduced to thirty years total.

The first five years of my sentence were cool. People from the street were sending me money, and I was getting a few visits. That always made the time fly, but the harsh reality is...When you're locked up, people will remember you for a while, but then, you get less letters, the money they send stops, and the visits slowly dwindle.

I'd spent thousands of dollars making sure that people around me were happy and having a good time my entire life. That's how I always was. If I was having a good time, I wanted everyone else to have a good time to. The last five years of my sentence, I didn't receive letters. What even hurt me more than that; I didn't get one visitor. For those five years, every one, except my mother and sister and a handful of friends, forgot about me. My mom and sister accepted my calls and sent me money from time to time, but nothing from anyone else.

As the months passed, the more forgiving I became. In 2010 I was sent to Morgantown, West Virginia. I'd finally become at peace with myself and at peace with my circumstances. News got to me that Uncle Ty suffered from a stroke while he was serving in Beckley Federal Correctional Institution in West Virginia right before he was released. Shortly after his release from prison, he suffered from another one. It tore me to pieces, but knowing that he was still alive was all that mattered. I couldn't take losing another family member.

In prison you meet people from all over, and really get to see how small the world is sometimes. There was this guy from Pittsburgh I met the last few months I was at Morgantown. He was a pretty good dude, everyone called him Pit because he was from Pittsburgh. He was serving twenty years on a dope charge. Anyway, as we started hanging out a little more, and he found out that I was from Hallsboro, he started asking me about certain people I knew. He'd lived in Raleigh and Greensboro for a few years off and on before he got sentenced.

He knew a lot of people from the area and one day we were talking, he asked me did I know a guy named Pogie and his cousin Stretch. I told him I did, and he told me what actually happened to Pogie. He knew what happened because he was actually fronting the guys the dope that Pogie and Stretch robbed. Small world.

I figured out that making things right didn't start the day I got out of prison. It started the very moment I made it up in my heart that I was a better person...

Society says that I've served my debt to it, but I can't expect anyone to absolve me for my wrongs...

I can say I'm sorry for the rest of my life, but that won't make up for missing my daughters' first day of school, seeing my sons throw a baseball for the first time, or for it taking so long for all of them to meet each other for the first time. That happened within the first six months of my release. It was one of the best days of my life.

I have to live with the fact that prison didn't take them away from me for all them years, my decisions did.

My father and I speak for fifteen minutes at a time over the phone now, maybe once a week. That's how long he's allowed to speak over the phone in prison. The only difference in our conversations now, we don't waste a second. We can't get back all those years we missed not having a father-son relationship, but now we're the best of friends. We never talk about the past, that's behind us. Some of the soundest advice I get now comes from my dad. On some of the craziest days of my life, he's the voice of reason that makes sense of it all.

I love Big Mike. He showed me that it's never too late to be a father. That's a lesson that makes more and more sense every time I see and speak to my children.

After all we've been through; it breaks my heart to see that some of society still glorifies drug dealers. If they knew what it feels like to lose the Rob Bases, the Joes, the people you lose while being locked in that box, especially the family members that mean the world to you; they'd reconsider who they celebrated.

As for me, day by day I grow. My definition of success is being a better man than I was yesterday. I have my challenges, we all do. I'll never be the man I once was. I'll never be the man I was on yesterday. I pray that my today's inspire someone's tomorrows in a positive fashion. That means more to me than anything else.

I guess happily-ever-after does exist. I found my happily-ever-after the day I forgave myself for all I've done. My tomorrows look a lot brighter now.

The End

SHOUT OUTS

Big shout to Hallsboro. I wouldn't want to be raised anywhere else. To all my people there, too many for me to name; thanks for raising me and holding me down.

Big shout out to Whiteville, Chadbourn, Bolton, Delco, East Arcadia, E-town, Clarkton, Myrtle Beach, poplar, Florence, Wilmington, Fayetteville, Shallotte, and all the surrounding areas that always have shown me love. My Raleigh peeps and all my cousins that live there, Kelvin Thurman, Johnny, Josh. Yeah...Kelvin you came through in a major way cuzzo.

In Durham, Lil' Lonnie, 'Lug man', love you man. Fred, Pee Wee, D.J Fatts, (Derrick Walls). I need you for that party. Bros. Three. No club can touch you!!! Lee Lee, holla at me. My whole Butner LSCI crew from Bull City-Hold it down.

Fayettenam (Fayetteville) –Shaboo, Big Zeke, Chip, Lenoir, Roderick, Dulo, D.P, Love. Queen City (I see you QC) Charlotte- Mike Jeffrey, Slow Fast, Chubb, Mike Sanders (keep writing them bangers homie). Mike Howe, I'm waiting on you lil homie.

Greenville, N.C- Sporty, Awaddalia, Salaam Bro. OG Brown.

New Bern- Hazzard Hawkins (I know you read, so pick up this one celly!!!)

Hickory, Asheville, Albermarle-Dontez (Blame Monkey). Mario Thomas (What's good home). Port City- PC Homes, Yuri Scott AKA 'Poke', Shady Grady, Main Man. Mont Mont, Steady B. It's a lot better on this side homie's, LET'S STAY OUT!!!! All my other PC Homes peeps. If I forgot you, forgive me, I have a lot on my mind.

ATL-Robert Glenn, Mike Childs, Robert Conner.Midwest, Ohio, Keith Lee.Louisville...Marve, Freddy Lee, Skully...what good? See yall soon. Indianapolis. ..Rick tha ruler, Jersey wat up. Gary Indiana what's up! Chi Town...Daryl Rodgers...D...Babybee! I'll be to see u n Texas soon! Tenn akey Nashville P.H...What's up celly? O, Vito, Pete...get at me.

Knoxville, Big Mike Taylor, Tae, J.D...Florida...MIA...Markee Taylor...hold your head fam! Detroit Mario Jones, Tito, Wild get at me. Kalamazoo...Bo Jones....told u I do big things lol...Brook what's up?

California Fukayana Ward...I'll be to see u! NY...Jenkins family...Michael Jenkins aka Siddiq and Dewanye Jenkins aka Saboor. Luv y'all! Can't forget u A.J.! Fats, Black Fred...Harlem stand up! Brooklyn, Bronx, Queens, Manhattan all my Fam there luv you guys. Jacob tha Jeweler...be to see u bro. We made out of there!

New Jersey... Jarrett Family luv u. Newark, Trenton, Jersey City, Edison. Philly...all my peps there luv y'all!

Special Thanks to Frank Logan, Steven 'ice'Gause Dedric Powell, E.B. Jeffery Gore. ..my club legends Family Smit, Thal, Spike, Tugg Gritt , Ice, Big Six, my lil Bro Markee, lil T, King Drett Powell, DJ Nut. VIP ENT u up next! Latoya Toe Kirksey...luv u girl! Marcelia tootie Gause and Marie Walker I can never repay yall for raising my kids....Thanks u so much!

All my peps behind that Iron curtain Feds N state....Hold your head! Its life after. Just keep dreaming and pursue your dream.

My story isn't to condone or glorify drugs or my actions. Actually it's to educate and help people understand that decisions can cost you! Decisions you make can derail you from becoming a productive person, for a very long time, possibly your entire life. Fortunately I've been given a second chance. With a lot of hard work, plus a good support system, things have been working out. So if there's a message to be obtained take the negative actions and decisions I've made and learn from them!

Michael Petey Powell.

www.ingramcontent.com/pod-product-compliance
Lightning Source LLC
Chambersburg PA
CBHW051415090426

42737CB00014B/2677